The 716
Ladies First

A.A. Lewis

Copyright © 2019 A.A. Lewis

All rights reserved. No part of this book may be reproduced in any form or by any electronic or mechanical means, including information storage and retrieval systems, without permission in writing from the publisher, except by reviewers, who may quote brief passages in a review.

The characters and events contained in this book are fictitious. Any similarities to real persons, living or dead and or events are coincidental and not intended by the author.

Credits for use of song titles belong exclusively to the artist named and or the producers and or writers of said songs and or album creators.

I do not own the rights to any music mention in this book.

Credits for cover design and images by Grafiz_Designs

Printed in the United States of America

Published by D & S Publishing

5047 W, Main St, Kalamazoo, MI 49009

sales@dspublishing.net

ISBN
978-1-68411-702-4 1-68411-702-X The 716 Hardcover
978-1-68411-703-1 1-68411-703-8 The 716 Paperback
978-1-68411-704-8 1-68411-704-6 The 716 eBook

Acknowledgment

When I decided that I could no longer hide behind the curtain of corporate America and claim that I was being my authentic self, I could not imagined how wonderful the freedom to be creative, to share my stories, thoughts and characters would be. I found it hard to believe that anyone would be interested, let alone would purchase my books. If you had told me that I would be conducting book discussions sessions with avid readers, and music enthusiasts that were able to take my vision to the next plateau by connecting the music to the story, the characters and seeing past what was written to help bring these fictional images to life, I would have called you a liar.

Our discussions, your text messages, emails and outreaches have warmed my heart and made me feel that this journey has been worth the steps I have taken to find my voice. With the conclusion of this part of The 716 Series, I hope that you will join me as I explore more of my creativity and diversity in writing. I promise to stay true to my urban roots, faithful to my culture, remain honest and raw in my delivery and above all represent the culture that help mold me into the woman, friend, mother, sister, and wife I am today.

So, to all the readers who took this journey with me- Thank you from the bottom of my heart. Your support means everything and more.

To the sisterhood that continues to build and empower- I am honored by your presence, your support, constant encouragement, the tears, laughs, struggles and love you've shown me. Whoever claims that the sisterhood is dead has not surrounded themselves with the cover melanin and royalty. I will gladly show them a crown that has been touched by the hands of queens guiding me to my throne. To Natasha, Liz, Trish, Lisa B. Rose, Tiffany Scott, Tiffany Hawkins, Tanya, CeCe, Shantell, Carlotta, Malisa, Shareece Robinson, Lanita, Nekeisha, Jennifer, Amina, Ashanti, Kenyatta, Evette, and Deana- Thank you all for making sure my slip wasn't showing and my crown sat high and straight. Thank you for being the support I need and proving that the sisterhood is alive and well.

To my family that showed me love from near and far. I hope I've made you proud! Your love and support motivates me to be better and to do amazing things with this gift I have been blessed with. Thank you Auntie Wanda, Auntie Ava, Auntie Valarie, and Auntie Carmella. You showed up to events, shared posts, encouraged and motivated me to keep going. I will always love you for seeing me through this journey, with your constant love and support.

I need to thank the women in Hip Hop and R &B, who influenced me way before I even realized that this vison had purpose. You are trailblazers for all of us. Through your music, we all have loved, cried, danced and dreamed. Your lyrics have helped us escape sorrow and pain, helped us see a better tomorrow and gave us hope. Without you these characters would not have been who they were, I would not have the courage to live through them and their experiences. So, to all the women artist that influenced the 1980's -2000's musical scene know that your essence moved me and helped make this dream a reality. Yall are dope as hell!

Last, but forever on my mind, to my husband, you are the lyrics to a Rakim song, doper than new adidas, you are a cool breeze on a hot summer day that finds it way between my thighs, you are the melody that my hips sashay to, the mood I relax on and the flavor red that quenches my thirst. YOU are the beat my heart echoes and plays like vinyl that a DJ spins. I will take any journey with you as long as you continue to love me the way that you do. Thank you for being my rock, cover and shield. Your support is unmeasurable, and your love is priceless. Thank you for all you do, so that I can be me.

A. A. Lewis

Table of Contents

Acknowledgment 3

Chapter One "Ladies First"- Queen Latifah 8

Chapter Two "Whoa"- Black Rob 12

Chapter Three "Buckingham Palace"- Canibus 17

Chapter Four "One Mic" –Nas 21

Chapter Five "Song Cry" - Jay Z 28

Chapter Six "U Don't Know Me"- T. I. 33

Chapter Seven "Oochie Wally" NAS 37

Chapter Eight "Stay Cool" -The Roots 42

Chapter Nine "Is That Your Chick"- Memphis Bleek 46

Chapter Ten "99 Problems"- Jay Z 54

Chapter Eleven "Snitches' - Master P / Snoop Dogg 58

Chapter Twelve "My Neck, My Back" – Khai 61

Chapter Thirteen "Oh Boy"- Cam'Ron 66

Chapter Fouteen "Da Baddest Bitch"- Trina 71

Chapter Fifteen "U Should've Known" Monica 78

Chapter Sixteen "Bring Em Out" -T.I. 82

Chapter Seventeen "Don't Say Nuthin'" - The Roots 85

Chapter Eighteen "True Love" - Faith Evan 89

Chapter Nineteen "Ante Up (Remix)"- M.O.P feat Busta Rhymes, Tephlon and Remy Ma 93

Chapter Twenty "Are You Still in Love with Me"- Keith Washington 95

Chapter Twenty-One "B K Anthem." – Foxy Brown 98

Chapter Twenty-Two "Get it Poppin"- Joe Budden 102

Chapter Twenty-Three "Breathe"- Fabulous 106

Chapter Twenty-Four "Illy"- T.I 108

Chapter Twenty-Five "ATF"- DMX 111

Chapter Twenty-Six "Izzo"- Jay Z 116

Chapter Twenty-Seven "I Ain't No Joke"- Eric B & Rakim 119

Chapter Twenty-Eight "Like You"- Bow Wow and Ciara 124

Chapter Twenty-Nine "Heaven Sent"- Keisha Cole 128

Chapter Thirty Let Me Hold You" Bow Wow Ft. Omarion 131

Chapter Thirty-One "Numb/ Encore" -Jay Z featuring Linkin Park 133

Chapter Thirty-Two "Hip Hop is Dead" – Nas 138

Chapter Thirty-Three "You don't Want Drama" *Ball & MJG 142

Chapter Thirty-Four "You can't play with my YoYo" – YoYo 149

Chapter Thirty-Five "Dangerously in Love 2"- Beyoncé 152

Chapter Thirty-Six "Bonnie and Clyde" Jay Z 157

Chapter Thirty-Seven "Crying out for me" – Mario 160

Chapter Thirty-Eight "Pass the Courvoisier" – Busta Rhymes 168

Chapter Thirty-Nine "Lean Back"- The Terror Squad 173

Chapter Forty "How You Gonna Act Like That "- Tyrese 179

Chapter Forty-One "Officially Missing You" –Tamia 185

Chapter Forty-Two "Complicated" - Robin Thicke 188

Chapter Forty-Three "No Idea's Original" – Nas 190

Chapter Forty-Four "Stay Down"- Mary J Blige 193

Chapter One
"Ladies First" - Queen Latifah

Anika

I must admit that I loved the way niggas and bitches looked at me. It wasn't a stare in disapproval or a judgmental look. It was almost one of reverence. I was standing on my own two feet. Not the way I had envisioned for myself, but nonetheless, I was standing and holding my head high. One never knows the true meaning of power until you have it. It has been damn near two years since my wedding day, and just as long since Que and Jay have been held over with no bond on some trumped-up charges. But when I said I do; I meant every word of it. That in sickness and health, richer or poorer vow shit wasn't supposed to happen so soon. I waited this long to be Mrs. Quincy Lamont Thomas, so there was no way I was going to let anyone, or thing stop me from supporting Que.

With Que and Jay temporarily out of the picture, some things have changed. In the past year and a half, it has been business as usual with one exception, I was now calling the shots. When everything went down the night of my wedding, The Board Members of The FAM scattered like roaches when the light comes on. Communication between them was scarce, but one thing was sure Brenneman told me, they had named me Que's successor. At first, I wasn't sure why. I didn't know the streets and the business-like Que and Jay did. Hell Yazz was better suited for the job than I was. Aunt Rose helped me see things from a different perspective. As much as my mother and father tried to shield me from our family business, I had always found myself somehow in the middle of it. Whether it be by accident or my sneaky ass planned it, I had grown up knowing more than I wanted to admit. I knew the operation enough to know the key players, the do's and don'ts, the faces and the money. I wasn't scared of protecting my own and getting what was mine. Most importantly, I knew the danger firsthand of not following the rules.

Aunt Rose had schooled me in what I called the art of the streets. I had never held a gun before, but now I was a pro. I could always command attention, only now no one dared step to me. One because I belonged to Que. Secondly, they knew who the fuck I was and the power that backed me. No one in their right mind would press up on me and my crew. When word got out that Que, Jay and Mario were gone, I had to make my presence known and quickly. When everything went down, most of the key players in the family were present at the wedding. Aunt Rose called a meeting so that we could set the record straight. She told Yazz and Monica to be there also. My lawyer Brenneman was also present. When all 55 of us summoned were present and accounted for, the solid Mahogany doors to the conference room located at Brenneman's law firm were closed. There were four armed guards posted outside of the room. We all sat in silence as Aunt Rose addressed the recent activities. You could see panic set in on the faces of a few individuals which was more alarming to me than anything. Que would always say, "you find out a lot about people when shit go wrong". And today I was definitely noticing the reality of his words.

When Aunt Rose was done speaking, I was introduced as the new head of The FAM, but not without backlash. It had been almost 50 years since a woman held this position, which was way before most of us in the room have been on this earth. But it was time. I allowed the whispers and idle chatter to continue long enough for these niggas to get it out of their system. With Aunt Rose by my side, I stood and addressed those present.

"We all heard what the wishes of The FAM are. You also know the consequences of acting in defiance of those wishes. I did not ask for this, hell I should be on my way to my honeymoon right now with the rightful heir to this throne, but here we are. Like many of you, upholding the legacy of The FAM is my top priority. A Priority that is not limited to just when things are going well. But right now when our integrity and loyalty is needed the most, when we stand the threat of outside interference, when our way of life is in jeopardy, you want to question why? We need to stand united now more than ever. We need to show the world who we are and the power we have. Most importantly we must not let anyone come between our way of life and the money we have. Que promised a reign of prosperity. Well, I'll honor that by making sure we all stay fed. I'm also proposing a reign of security. What happen to Que and Jay should have never happened. Mario should have never had to die. NO MORE. Enough is enough. With me at the head of this table, we will do things differently, we will continue to grow the territory and we will do it in a way that no one will ever see it coming. And by the time they do, it will be too late. I need your support. I need your wisdom and strength. More importantly, Que would want, no Que would expect you to. I was born a member of this family. There is no way in hell I would ever let the reputation of The FAM die under my watch. Blood may bring us together, but money and power will keep us united." I stated firmly as one by one they pledged their allegiance.

I was ready. It was time. I could no longer deny who I was or the family I was born into. I could not afford to play the innocent naive role anymore. There was too much at stake. Que needed me. My sons depended on me. And The FAM had me. Finally, all the power I ever wanted, and the ability to influence change. I was ready to take my seat and eat at the head of the table.

Chapter Two

"Whoa"- Black Rob

Anika

There were two sides to me. I played the doting mother to Rockmond and Draymond. I loved being a mom. It was a role I was born to play. I did not mind the smelly diapers, breastfeeding, or the way those two woke up in the middle of the night wanting to play. I had always dreamed of having children someday and I was fortunate to give birth to twins. Rockmond or Roc as I called him was the firstborn by 4 minutes and 20 seconds. He reminded me of his father every time he demanded something of me. It was always now with a sense of urgency. He was already used to getting his way. Draymond or Dray as I called him, was very mild-tempered and just like his brother, had his father's intense eyes. He seemed to be focused and driven. Which sometimes as the younger brother is not always the best trait to have.

There were playdates, mommy and me swim classes, plus visits to see my mom on a regular basis. We were the perfect picture with one exception. Que was missing. Que spoke to them every chance he got. I made sure that they knew who their father was and the sound of his voice. I could tell being away from them broke Que's heart but he's adamant about never bringing them to visit him in prison. No matter how much I wanted for him to see them, Que was not having it. He told me that no son of his would ever see the insides of the cement block on his watch. That it was unnatural to see black men caged up like animals. It was an image that once you see it you can't un-see it. Yet sad to say, it was more common than not.

In the year that Que had been locked up, the boys had grown so much. There were milestones after milestones as the two of them tried outdoing each other. If one crawled the other one walked. If one started speaking, the other one would start reading. Yes reading. They were the joys of my life and the peace that kept me focused especially right now. I knew with them exactly who I was and what they demanded from me. And I was more than willing to oblige.

Then there was the B side of the record. That is my other life dedicated to the streets. I would comb through the streets making myself known and seen. The attention and power at first was overwhelming, but before long I was used to it. I was that bitch other girls hated on and the chick every dude wanted to fuck. But I was off-limits. They all knew who the fuck I was and who I represented. They could hate, but I knew it was just jealousy. From the clothes to the jewelry, to the cars, I stayed jiggy. Hair was never out of place, and my nails always manicured to perfection. There wasn't anything the twins and I didn't have that I wanted. I flossed every time I left the house, especially when I was conducting business. I don't overdo it, just enough to let mutharfucka's know my name. I was the baddest bitch in town and I had the power to back it up. You know how you would buy a cassette tape, album or CD, play the hell out of the song they have in heavy rotation on the radio but never listen to the other songs. Only to find out the song you skipped over was the shit! That song was way better than the song you originally purchased the cassette tape, CD or album for. Well, I'm that song you always used to skip. I just wasn't Que's wife anymore but the queen on the chessboard.

While everyone was so preoccupied with my looks, phat ass and thighs, or my perky breast, I was running a business like a multi-million-dollar conglomerate. I had moved the business of The FAM more mainstream. I had legitimized about a third of all operations. Now don't get me wrong, The FAM has always been well organized and diverse in our dealings. But what I was able to do is take that to the next level. Yeah, we owned real estate, businesses and of course the streets. When I say next level shit, I'm talking about, hotels, manufacturing businesses, contributing to political campaigns, having a stock portfolio that rivalled those of the top 3% of this country. I had invested in start up's that were paying at a good return rate. I had managed to clean up our image on the streets so that our signature style was not so noticeable. I was able to buy back most of the corner stores in the city. Yeah, the front man was the Armenians and Middle Easterners which further continued to add to the cover of our operations. They gave the visual of being the owners of the stores, but The FAM ran things. I was able to place our product in the stores and off the street corners. Customers could walk into any number of stores and purchase whatever high suited their need.

I was able to launder money faster and more efficiently than ever before. With Breneman's assistance, I had managed to buy a few franchises throughout the territory. We had fast food, car washes, laundromats, car dealerships and even prepaid cell phone shops. Every connect I could think of that we used to move weight, I bought. I even invested in a company specializing in spyware. The technology that they had kept us informed on new strategies the government was using to detect drugs and other criminal activity. There I was sitting at their table taking in the very knowledge they would be hoping to take me down with. I was playing chess and controlling the board. Every move a calculated ploy to stay on top and in control. Two steps ahead of the game with eyes in the back of my head. I wanted to know and see what was coming at us from all directions. The things my father told me were all making sense. It was his street knowledge and wisdom along with Aunt Rose that kept me focused on the big picture. I didn't ask for this life, but dammit this shit had me playing the hand I was dealt and winning.

Being a mother came first, but close behind was the streets. Aunt Rose stressed the need for me to get my team in order right away. So right after I was appointed, I began weeding through the profiles of everyone in The FAM. If I was going to do this, I needed to make sure I had people in charge that respected me the way they did Que. I knew I had their allegiance, but I needed to make sure those reporting to me had The FAM's, as well as my best interest at all times. So it was without hesitation that Yazz be my Right Hand. She had shown her loyalty to The FAM and Que even at the cost of her life. She was intelligent, and hood. I knew that with Jay being locked up, Yazz needed something to take her mind off of him, plus she was no-nonsense. With her by my side, I knew the boys and I were in good hands.

When it came to Monica, Aunt Rose was not sure if she could manage running the streets alone. Monica was gully, but could she be grimy was the question. Could she do what was needed and walk away. I knew she was capable, hell Que trusted her, but could she be the one to pull the trigga if needed? Aunt Rose suggested that I make Monica and my cousin Sleepy co-chairs of the street. This would mean that everyone reported directly to those two. Monica could learn more about the business side of things and Sleepy could be groomed to fill the void Mario's death caused. It made sense to me. Sleepy was my first cousin on my mother's side of the family. He was two years older than me. Que had placed him in charge of the territory West of Michigan. Everyone knew Sleepy and just like Que they had a fear of letting him down. At my wedding was the first time I'd seen him in years. He was handsome, dark-skinned and well built. When he approached Que and me at the reception, he flashed the prettiest smile of white perfectly lined teeth. It was the smile that used to greet me as a kid whenever I would visit the Fruitbelt. He was also the same cousin that would come to my defense whenever Que would mess with me or anyone else for that matter. I knew I could trust him, just like I trusted him all those years ago. And with everyone else in place, the new leadership was presented, and we had set course on a new journey of controlled chaos and mayhem in the streets of Buffalo.

Chapter Three
"Buckingham Palace"- Canibus

Yazz

Anika's move to modernize the FAM was a great move. It classed up the operation and gave the appearance that business was legit. I could walk around in Prada and Gucci looking cute and not look out of place. Not that anyone would try me, but nothing said trouble more than me walking into a trap house in stiletto's rockin the latest gear and bussin' shots off to prove a point. At least, for the most part, I could be chill. Hair done, nails polished, all while keeping my finger on the trigger.

I was due to make a few rounds to check on shit. Monica and Sleepy had things under control, but it was good for the streets to still see me. After all I was Jay in female form. I had been around him long enough to mimic his every step. All that time together I had studied the teacher and now I could flip that shit and become the leader. Every move I made reminded me of Jay. At night I would wear his t-shirt to keep him close to me and his scent surrounded me in comfort. I handled business with ease. I knew being the face and right hand to Anika meant that I could not just move reckless. So I played the calm role. Walked around lookin like that kinda girl, knowing all along I could take any muthafucka's life that tried me.

"Yazz, I'm not asking, I'm telling you," Anika commanded with new confidence. I hated when she was right. I knew that I needed to go see Jay. My heart just could not bring me to see him like this. It had been almost two years since I was able to hold him in my arms. We went from partyin' at the reception to my whole world being turned upside down. It took everything in me to hold it together. At first, everyone kept saying Jay and Que would be home soon. That we had nothing to worry about. Shit every time they went before the Judge it seemed like the whole world was against them. I felt like after all that had happened, destiny just wasn't going to let us be together. It broke my heart seeing him like that. I know he needs me, but I need him and not in his current state. Hell, fuck what me and Jay goin' through, I don't know how Anika is able to hold it together the way that she does. Maybe it was that slap to the face Aunty Rose gave her when everything was going down. Whatever it was Anika was BOSS in every sense of the word now.

I pulled up to the Erie County Holding Center. Its hard cold exterior was laced with neatly trimmed bushes and flower beds. I thought there was nothing perfect nor happy about this place. I parked the car inhaled and begin to open the driver side door. I held the door handle and just sat there thinking of Jay and how I missed his face, that smile and the way his eyes spoke to me. I tried to open the door, but my heart would not allow me to. I could hear the soft side of me begging to go in and see him, but my rough exterior would not budge. A mix of emotions engulfed me and before I knew what was happening, I had driven off in the direction I had just come from.

"FUCK THIS SHIT! I screamed as tears rolled down my face.

I knew he would forgive me, but I just could not bring myself to see him like this and my heart could not take the rejection those steal cold bars placed on my soul. Anika would just have to yell at me again, but I'm sure it will come at a greater cost.

I got out of there so fast. There was no way I was gonna see Jay locked up like that. The first few times I had visited I told myself he would be home soon. But then weeks turn into months and before I knew it, a year had passed. The law states that defendants are supposed to be guaranteed a speedy trial, but in the case of Jay and Que there wasn't anything fair or speedy about this process. They were holding him on some trumped-up charges. Everyone there knew that these murder charges would not stick. There was no way in hell they had any sort of reliable witness nor evidence to support such a claim. Brenneman told us since bail was denied, Jay and Que had to stay in jail until the trial. The whole ordeal was bullshit. Just thinking about it made my blood boil.

As I drove back into the city limits, I was thinking of all the wrongs that have gone down over the past year. It was too much for me emotionally to invest in. At this stage in the game, I would rather catch logic instead of emotions. I had no time for tears. There was business to handle and the streets had no love for a bitch carrying her heart on her sleeve. I did that already and look where it got me. I agreed silently with myself as I pulled into the gun range on Niagara Falls Blvd. This was the best way for me to release stress. It was better than me taking out my frustrations on some crackhead feignin for the rock, or me cussing out a youngin for not slangin' harder. This was me controlling my emotions. This was me staying focused. This was me staying calm. Besides nothing felt more at home to me them bussin' off a few rounds.

"You're becoming a pure natural at this" the white burly man behind the counter commented as he checked my board results. I had impressed myself. I had grown from being a wild child to a professional gun handler.

My aim had improved. I could handle the kickback. And most important I had respect for my piece. I had wrapped up my session and decided to head back to my house. I wasn't hungry just tired. Mentally tired. Before I could even pull out the parking lot good, the car phone rang.

What" I answered as I listen to the caller on the other line.

"I'm on my way" I replied. This may be the break we need I thought as I made a left and headed back towards Buffalo. "I just might be able to bust off some more of this negative energy after all," I said aloud as the bass pounded through the truck while the music and the thought of holding my piece sent shocks to my body.

Chapter Four

"One Mic" –Nas

Que

Knuckles on the cold concrete. Twenty, forty, sixty. My mind could not be any clearer and more focused than it was at this moment. I had one goal; to get back to my family. Business would handle itself, but I made promises that I do not intend on breaking. Eight… Ninety… My sons needed me, and I needed them. My queen had risen to the top and I was fuckin stuck behind this cage like a fuckin animal. One hundred. I wasn't new to this shit. I had been in County before. But not like this. I needed to keep my cool and remain focused. There was only one goal, one plan. Everything else was minor. Twenty… Thirty… I breathed as I clenched my teeth locking my jaw with a hardened look on my face. It was all I could do not to punch the wall. Pushing my weight upon my knuckles and catching my breath, eyes dead ahead. Sixty, seventy…I could only imagine what Anika looked like. Holding her in my arms was the only thing that would comfort me at this moment. To hear her voice, to touch her and smell her hair. It had become the small things a nigga take for granted that had me waiting to see the sky and bathe in the lights of the street. Eighty… Ninety, two hundred. It was a tap on the shoulder from Jay that broke my stride. I had done two hundred push-ups and could go another hundred without even thinking about it.

"Thomas, you got a visitor," The guard said.

Behind these walls, you can easily lose track of time. I completely forgot today was Tuesday. Anika usually rolled up here on Tuesday, Thursday and Saturday. It was the only highlight to my existence right now. I lived vicariously through her. She was handling business. I have to admit I was impressed. Anika had owned her rightful place within the family. This was not the way I had imagined it, hell none of this shit, but nothing pleased me more than knowing that while I was here, she was holding it down out there. I thought to myself as I took the walk through the cell blocks, and cages with other niggas, soldiers being held down by the lack of opportunity and a good lawyer. Most of these niggas didn't stand a chance. They were either waiting to be sentenced or gettin' ready to ride out on the next bus to their permanent home depending on the sentence. I knew that someday I would have to pay for my sins, but I always thought it would be a bullet and not a false fuckin' case that would send me to hell.

I heard the doors lock and slam behind me. The only saving grace was that money talks. The guards were willing to look out if their pockets got paid. That was an easy fix. Anika had paid off guards and kept both Jay's and my commissary stocked. We ruled like kings among soldiers in this bitch. Our reps preceded us. Everyone wanted acted as if they knew us, like just because we were behind bars, we were family. Shit, I'm sure that under the circumstances we were all one in the same. The streets had eaten us up and spit us out. It had been the only life we knew. It didn't matter whether it was the drug game, being the stick up kids, carjackin', or just out here shootin' up shit, we were all victims of the same fate. And at some point, we would all have to answer for our lot in life. Some sooner than others. The closing of another door slammed behind me as I heard another guard yell for clearance.

I had finally reached what I could only describe as a piece of heaven in hell. Anika had arranged for her and I to have a room to ourselves. It wasn't much but it was ours. It was a chance for me to hold her in my arms, a chance to feel her lips on my lips and love her even if it was a temporary fix to my addiction to her. There was only a table and two chairs but it was more than enough for me. There were no windows, just concrete blocks lining the walls like the basement of an old house. Cracks and peeling paint decorated the corners of the room and exposed pipes probably covered with asbestos. I would breathe my death if it meant having a chance to see Anika without the restraints of bars and plexiglass covered in old handprints and stale lipstick. The guard uncuffed me, smiled and exited the room. The door opened from the other corner of the room.

Watching Anika walk-in reminded me of our wedding day. She was my vision of perfection. It wasn't even that she had to try to be sexy she just was. There was a confidence that had taken over her and made me want her even more. I held her in my arms as we kissed hard and long. The taste of her tongue as it slipped in and out of my month sent shocks throughout my body. We could spend time talking, but I knew what she needed. She knew what I needed. And with our time being limited to whatever those bastards gave us not one moment would be wasted. Anika has undressed and stood there in an all-red lace thong and bra combo. Her body was just as I remembered. With her high heels still on she walked over to me and squatted and began to suck and stroke me back to my former self. It was something about the way she took me in and wrapped her heart-shaped lips around my dick that even under the harsh fluorescent light looked sexy as hell. I held her head gently as she stroked back and forth, back and forth. My dick was hard and ready. It had been weeks since we were able to be alone. And just the scent of her put my mind at ease. She was my escape from everything I knew. She was all that was right in my fucked-up world.

I watched as she inhaled me and blew on the mass of my cock as it glided in and out of her stretched month. Her lips were glossed over and shined as she went up and down my shaft leaving traces of glitter along the path. It took everything in me not to bust as she relaxed my mind and created a sense of normalcy for me. Anika controlled me. With her sexiness, her class and her smarts. There was no way I could just let this bull shit I found myself in deny me my rightful spot by her side. I could tell that she missed me. With each stroke, she moaned and spoke to me. Her sounds set off a hypnotic melody that one could easy rest peacefully too.

I grabbed Anika by the waist and mounted her on my waist. Holding only her plump ass, I began to rock her onto my swollen dick. Anika loved it when I gave it to her like that. She would ride me while looking into my soul. She bounced up and down as I gripped her sticky body leaving impressions of my fingerprints on her. She would rock and I would pull, and she would roll, and I would moan. She would whisper in my ear only things that were meant for me to hear as I focused on stroking her with my piece. I watched as she climaxed over and over exhausting herself but unwilling to surrender. I gently pulled her off me and hoisted her up on my shoulder facing me. I could feel her heartbeat pulsating through her veins. She sat there legs draped over my back holding on to my head as I slowly began to lick the center of her universe. It was just like I remembered. It was the sweetness of honey that flowed from her. With each lick, I drove my tongue deeper and deeper into her. I could feel her thighs tightened as I set off alarms within her. Anika would kick and scream out in pleasure and I sucked and licked every piece of her inner being. It was the only food I needed and for what seemed like an eternity I had been deprived of it. I took what was mine as Anika lay exhausted in my arms. I had kissed every inch of her body in my dreams and there was no way I would not take advantage of this opportunity to make my dreams come true. Her lifeless body hung over the side of the table as I entered her from the back. The arch her body gave mimicked a cat stretching to excitement. She held the table as I pounded her pussy from the back. She was wet and tight, and her lips wrapped around my dick like I was the key designed to open her up. Her legs spread open, back arched and standing in her pumps Anika bucked back with every thrust of my manhood I gave her. Her ass shook with jealousy causing me to slap it whenever the rhythm caught me.

I did not care who was watching or even if someone was listening, I would not be denied the pleasures of being with my wife. She was the only addiction I had known and in my deepest sorrow the only cure for the pain. She needed me and I longed for her. Her pussy kept me sane and I needed it for fear of losing my mind. Anika bounced on that dick like a champ and took every inch I had pounded into her. She was and had always been the perfect woman for me. I could not hold on any longer as my cries and moans overcame the room, before I had known it, Anika had released herself from my grip and had opened wide to catch every drop of my cum in her mouth. It was warm, wet and the perfect end to a fucked-up situation.

Anika and I knew we only had a few more minutes to be together.

"Que, did you hear what I said," Anika asked.

"I got you, shorty." I replied.

"How would you like me to handle this?" Anika continued.

I looked at her, and I knew she got what I was saying with no words spoken. That is just how close Anika and I were. She understood my nonverbals and I knew she would act accordingly.

"Que, I really think you should allow me to ..." Anika started to speak.

"I already told you, NO SONS of Mine will see the inside of this shitty place, NOT NOW NOT EVER! Even if it is just to visit." I interrupted with force.

I could tell the look on Anika's face was pure disappointment. Fuck that bull shit. I only get one chance to be a father and I'll be damned if it starts with them seeing me locked up in a cage. I did not want this life for them and shit, here we are. Seeing them here would just be too much for me. My priority was not being in this cage, but back home on the streets making sure my family was safe.

"Anika listen, baby, I didn't mean to yell. But you know how I feel about this shit." I spoke breaking the silence. "I just don't want this for them, hell, I didn't want it for you and here we are. I'll be home soon enough. I promise." I added

"You know what Que, don't promise me anything else. Make that shit happens sooner than later," she stated looking me square in the eyes with a straight face.

I understood the look. She had given it plenty of times before. She had become a great study. My baby had BOSSED up and all I wanted to do was get out of here and share the throne with her.

Just then the door opened, and the guard called my name. I knew what that meant. Anika watched as they came in and cuffed me. It was becoming an all too familiar scene. Before I exited the room, I looked back at Anika and yelled, "YAZZ BETTER BE HERE WITH YOU NEXT TIIME AND YOU CAN TELL HER IT'S NOT AN ASK IT'S A COMMAND"

The door closed behind me and the walk back to the cellblock was just as cold and alone as the journey there. Brenneman better find a way out of this shit before I do, because there will be hell to pay if I have to take too many more walks like this.

Chapter Five

"Song Cry" - Jay Z

Jay

Que left out the cell for one of his weekly visits with Anika. I laid on the bunk facing the ceiling. I counted the chips, cracks and imperfections that outlined the 4X8 cage that was my temporary home. The walls were a dingy white. And the floors were just as cold as the steel bars that flowed through the buildings. I laid there thinking about Yazz. All the promises I had made her. The life I wanted to give her vs. the world I birthed her into. She deserved better. I was a good dude in a fucked-up shituation. All I wanted was to see her face. Her smile gave me hope. I needed it. I needed her. I could feel my jaw clenching shut. I knew her reasoning for not being here, as fucked up as It might be I didn't blame her. Still that didn't mean that it didn't hurt.

As the weeks turned into something else and the visits became sparser, I could see it in her eyes. I had become evil and the cause of everything wrong in Yazz's life. Even if she didn't blame me, I did. I knew this life was not for her. From that shit in Michigan, to how she had been moving since we came back to Buffalo. I should have stopped it then. But I didn't. I knew then, but my pride wouldn't let me say no to her. I should have turned her away and called it quits when Que and I had to leave the city; and now look. If I could just see her face. If I could just hear her voice. I would be able to tell just how far gone she was, whether there was still a chance for me to right some wrongs. "Damnit!" I said out loud as my fist hit the wall.

I have done some small time before with Que, but this by far has been the hardest. Before Yazz, ain't none of those bitches ever have my heart. There was one that came close back in college. Other than that, Yazz has always been the woman for me. I knew it from the day we met, even though I didn't show it. Had me wishing I never made that move. I should've stuck with my guts. I knew the streets and what they would do to you, your relationships and those you loved. But there was just something about her. My soul had never known the type of peace and unselfish love she had shown me. I knew Yazz still had feelings for me, somewhere deep down. The question was would she be ok doing this bid with me if it came down to it. The bigger question is did I have the right to even ask her to do that if and when judgment came down.

I paced back and forth wondering what she was doing. I knew this was not healthy. When you're surrounded by niggas and concrete your mind wonders to the bright and beautiful spots in life and Yazz was just that for me. Her smile would light up a room and the way she moved those long legs had a nigga wishing he knew better. Did better. The truth was I felt like I was losing the one thing I needed in this world the most. It was never about the sex with Yazz. We had that real emotional connection. She stimulated my mind. Had ya boy thinking about life after this shit. That I could have love, a family and forget about all the bad shit I've done. She made me forget about my past transgressions and she never questioned or frowned on what I did or who I was. She had accepted me for who I was, an educated thug nigga. Yet she wanted me. Encouraged me and loved me. Or at least she used to. As I sit in this cold cell, I just didn't know any more.

It was rec time. I chose to go hang out in the gym, maybe catch a game of basketball. It had been a while since I played. But I was confident that my All-State and All-American skills would still be evident once I got on the court. Back in the day, I played basketball for Turner Carroll High School. I was deemed Buffalo's great black hope. I had recruiters coming to see me play from across the country. I was destined for greatness. There was even talk about my one day being an NBA great. There was not a team in the city nor conference that could hold us. I was the point guard no one wanted to check. I had mad skillz. I could ball with the street niggas at the park, but I had the fitness and the coachability that talent scouts looked for that made me a hot commodity. I was deemed the best b-ball player Buffalo had seen since Cliff Robinson.

Niggas everywhere knew my game. Everyone wanted to ball with me. Saturdays I would play at Delaware Park. Every Nigga in the city that thought they had game would be there. Not to mention the honeys. The courts would be packed with anyone willing to showcase their talents or cuties looking for a come up. Occasionally there would be guest appearances from NBA stars. I remember this one time this kid, a rookie that had just entered the NBA. He was recruited to come down with a few of his boys to play with us. Now outside of Rucker's Park in NYC, Delaware Park was the next big shit. So, it was no surprise that Rookies and NBA greats came to watch or flex their skillz on the court. Any who, this nigga rookie got mad cause I was embarrassing his ass on the court. Nigga started getting aggressive. Came at me hard in the paint and fouled me nasty while I was up in the air. Had I not had skillz, I could have really injured myself. This bum ass nigga gone get mad cause I was schooling him, and he supposed to be making crazy loot in the NBA. I could tell by his demeanor he had an attitude. He was talkin mad shit, but I was breakin' that niggas ankles. The crowd of onlookers was laughing and started clowning him. I was dribbling the ball up the court when he said next move I make he gone foul the shit out of me, to which I replied, then I'mma embarrass yo wack ass then blast yo bitch ass in the face with the rock. And as promised that nigga tried it and I'm true to my word, so when the ball hit him straight deadass in the face it should not have been a surprise.

Next thing I know this bitch wanna charge at me like a little girl whose feelings are hurt. What he didn't know or must have forgot, is that I ain't that nigga. My crew always been tight. Que and I ran together since day one. He was more street than me and I was more studious than him, but together nobody could stop us. Que pulled that gun out so fast; Mr. NBA Star shit his pants. Not only did that calm his ass down real quick, but it gave everyone a chance to see that Que, myself and our crew wasn't shit to fuck with. We were young niggas in the FAM's dynasty, but we were a force to be reckoned with. Shidd, that nigga game hadn't been the same since that day, and I think he went on to have a wack ass career in the league, couldn't have lasted more than 3 seasons, being traded twice as many times. I laughed as I reminisce about that shit as the ball went swish into the net.

It wasn't before long a convict game of basketball was underway. Of course, my team was up. There was a lot of trash talkin' name callin', but that never bothered me. At the end of the game, we all knew what the fuck happens. A muthafucka either on the winning side of things or you lose. I hadn't lost since I picked up the ball, and just because I was behind bars didn't stop the winning streak. But you know there is always a nigga in the bunch with something to prove. Other dudes already knew of me or had heard of me. Not just my basketball skillz, but who I represented. Niggas would get the fuck out of my way when they saw me coming. Even here, my rep had preceded me. But there is always one. One nigga who wanna try some shit, one nigga that want to take that chance, one asshole who wanna try you thinking he will make a name for himself. And if I wasn't having it before, it damn sure wasn't gonna happen in here.

I was going up for a layup, and this bitch nigga try to under-cut me while I'm up in the air. Again, had I not had skillz, this could have been a problem. I brushed it off, it's a good game of convict ball and hell, we still winning. I had peeped this niggas game though, I had brushed off the first time, but my pride would not let that shit fly again. He even looked like he was up to something. I was going to have to show him how I get down. Just like clockwork, this nigga tried it. I could see in his eyes he was gunnin' for me and I was waiting. Instead of going up for the easy layup, I swung the ball and hit that nigga dead in the face. Before he knew it, I landed my fist in the space the basketball had not occupied. I could not stop. My fist connected one after another with his face. Something inside of me had snapped. I tried to stop, but I couldn't. This nigga needed to learn who the fuck I am or.. was it Yazz that needed to…? I thought to myself as I began to snap out of my fit of rage and Que was pulling me off of him. I heard the whistles of the guards blowing and the alarms blaring as Que pulled me away from the nigga that lay helpless on the old unpolished court. My hands were bloody and my once crisped white tee had stains of life on it; painted with that niggas DNA. One inmate quickly took off his shirt and gave it to me for me to change into. He put the shirt I had on so that by the time everything had settled, he was being walked down to the hole. It had happened so fast, and I'm not even sure what happen. All I know was that it should have been me going to the hole. Maybe there I could learn to forgive myself for all the shit I had done. Maybe then Yazz could forgive me too.

Chapter Six

"U Don't Know Me"- T. I.

Sleepy

It felt weird as fuck to be back in the B-Lo. I had been gone for 10 years and for good reasons. I left just like when Que and Jay got rushed out, some shit had gone down and I was at the heart of it. Nonetheless, I was back. When Que told me he might need me to handle some bidness, he knew I would come running. Besides, when I got the invite to the wedding of my cousin Anika to Que, there was nothing that would have prevented me from standing up for them at their wedding. Hell, it was about time he got caught. And there wasn't anyone better suited for love than those two. I wasn't sure how long I would be back in Buffalo, but I came prepared. Besides, home is where you lay your head and in this life, you be lucky to wake up day to day in order to have somewhere to call home.

I rode around the city becoming more familiar with my surroundings. The hood had changed since the last time I was here. Old landmarks were gone and replaced with new images. One thing that did not change was the players and the game. My job was to make sure that shit stayed the same.

Aunty Rose gave specific instructions for me to follow. And with no hesitation, I would carry that shit out. There were familiar faces in crowds, but for all they knew, I was new to Buffalo. I kept to myself, which was just the way I liked it. There were several things Que and Jay taught me about this game. My crew was small. Everyone else was just associates. If they weren't working for the FAM, they were expendable. Cash Rules Everything Around Me, and nothing could be truer than when it came to how I moved. I appreciated the ride Anika had delivered to my apartment, but it was too flashy for my taste. I preferred my all black Expedition. The tints on the truck were just dark enough but within guidelines. I didn't have amps spilling out base every time I rolled around. It was real lowkey but still made a statement. Besides, the less people know, the better. The truck did the job, I got from point A to fuckin B with no problem.

I rode around checking on the trap houses, corner stores and handling any business needed. For all they knew I was just another soldier. I usually let Monica play the role. Her loud ass was perfect for that shit. I looked just like the muscle, Monica's bodyguard. We were the Bonnie and Clyde of the streets. I was teaching her the game from the inside. Until now Monica just did what Que and Jay needed her to do. She was an order taker. Now she was learning how to make the calls. How to demand respect and keep it. It wasn't by being obnoxious and flashy, but by the silent moves she made. Sometimes the scariest shit was the nigga that didn't say anything. She was learning how to be observant, aware of her surrounding, read niggas, not just fuck'em. But to understand their next move and anticipate the outcome so you stay one step ahead of them. Monica was a great study. She caught on quick. It was gettin to the point where I was comfortable with her by my side, more importantly, I knew she had my back. And a nigga like me don't let that guard down that easy.

The one thing I knew for sure was that this arrangement was bidness and bidness only. Don't get me wrong, Monica was fine as hell. Shiiid, the way she rolled and licked that blunt, I could only imagine what she would do with the real thing, but this was money. And nothing fucked with me tryna get paid. I kept that shit separate, besides, nothing good came of mixing the two. We had present-day examples that proved that.

Hell Anika and Que might be the first, might. I knew Monica's ass heard me when I explained the rules of our relationship, but that didn't stop her from trying a nigga. She would wear them coochie cutter shorts with her ass all out, a pair of heels with a tank top and no bra. It looked sexy as fuck, and damn near made it hard to stay focused especially when they would bounce in the car. It was shit like that, that had me keep my distance from Monica. She thinks I'm an angry nigga mad at the world, but the truth was it was for her protection and mines. We were a team and this was bidness homie.

I was headed to this one spot to make a run. It was not that far from Charlie Fatburger on Delavan and Grider. After making the run, I stopped and ordered some food. I sat at the furthest end of the spot facing the door and the big wall window. I was wearing a black fitted cap, a nice sized gold chain hung around the crew neck of my white polo tee and a pair of black jeans. A custom pair of Black Timberlands finished my outfit off. They were designed with the skyline of NYC on them in white, grey and blue. I was feeling calm and collected until some wannabe nigga's bitch started smiling in my direction. She was cute. He must have felt some kinda way cause this nigga got loud and started to approach me. Now I'm not that nigga you wanna try and ain't no pussy worth fighting over. I was about to get up when I heard my order be called. He must've seen the look on my face, and he hesitated.

"We Got a problem"? I asked with my teeth clenched. Lifting my tee just enough to show my nine strapped to my side.

"Nah Bruh, No Problem" he uttered as his wack ass sat back down in his seat.

I grabbed my order and walked out of the restaurant. I place my food in the seat and calmly posted outside of my truck. I could see him yelling and carrying on with his girl. I watched as they grabbed their order and headed in my direction. I walked to the passenger side door and opened it not taking my eyes off of her. She had tears in her eyes. This nigga was too busy carrying on like a little hoe, that he missed how I silently macked on his girl. I nodded to the open door and winked. She took one look at him and again at me. The choice was obvious to me. She could either ride with that wannabe nigga or come get with a real ass player. The choice was hers and from the smile that crept across her face, I could tell she made the right decision. She walked with a sense of urgency as she hopped into the passenger side of my truck. He stood there calling her all kinds of bitches and hoes. I gestured once again by silently flashing the nine-piece strapped on my side and the other hand across my lips as if to tell that nigga to shh. There he stood speechless and dumbfounded as I drove off with his bitch and food. These niggas weren't ready. The players had changed but not the game. It was good to be back home. Good food and fine ass bitches. Yeah, things had changed since I left, but one thing for sure is a wack ass nigga will always be a wack ass nigga.

Chapter Seven

"Oochie Wally" NAS

Monica

I played on the pole as Tre', Brian and Sam all watched. The high from the blunt had me feeling good as hell and horny as fuck. I did a twirl on the pole that ended with me clappin' my ass on the floor in a split. A shower of ones fell over me. The room was filled with smoke that kept the contact high going. I stepped off the stage and took the blunt from Tre' and puffed as I grinded on his lap while facing him. I made rings of smoke clouds as he cupped my ass and grinded with me. I could feel his dick begging to be released from his basketball shorts. Adina Howard played in the background and all I could think of was their t-shirts and my panties about to come off. I stood up and allowed Sam to remove my panties with his teeth. He took his fingers and gently massaged my clit as I rocked back and forth to the music. I puffed the blunt and let out moans of satisfaction. Tre had begun to kiss my back and neck. He stood behind me and I could feel his hard cock pressed into the lower part of my back. Tre' had planted his mouth in my pussy causing me to shake as he drank my juice as it poured out of me. Brian was standing jerking his dick watching as the other two got me nice and wet and ready to ride his dick.

Tre smacked my ass as he entered it. I was mounted on Brian's hard dick and had managed to inhale Sam like he was the next blunt I wanted to smoke. In unison they stroked me. Filling each of my Orpheus's, pushing my body to ecstasy. Nothing gave me greater joy than feeling pain and pleasure at the same time. Each of them brought something new and exciting to my craving for sex. So, when I asked them about joining me tonight, I could tell they were hesitant, but I assured them I would make it worth their while. Besides who would give up an opportunity like this. I figured if their wives weren't willing, I was always down. You heard me. These niggas all had wives. But that didn't stop them from eating my pussy and going home and kissing their wives. I smiled thinking of how good it felt as they fucked me. Brian's dick was so deep inside me, he touched every sensitive spot causing me to cum repeatedly. This excited Tre, as he stroked my ass. Both my pussy and ass was tight. It didn't matter how big a dick I took, It always went right back to the perfect tightness which always drove men wild. Sam stroked my mouth as I played with his balls with my right hand. I took all of him in without gagging. I could tell he was getting close to cumming. He grabbed my head and forced strong strokes down my throat. I opened wide as he hand stroked his thick creamy cum out of his dick and into my mouth. I took it all in and slowly let it drip out of my mouth and back onto his dick and sucked it all off to swallow it. It was also at the moment that Tre was ready to explode. His pace had picked up as he let out a cry of completion and satisfaction. Brian would not be outdone. Now that he had me to himself he flipped me over and took my pussy from the back. With every thrust, I bucked back. This dick was thick and long, which gave me the confidence to buck wild and hard. I knew he would not slip out of my wet pussy. Sam and Tre both watched in amazement at the act Brain and I performed. He held me as my back made the perfect arch for him to enter in and out of me with ease. I would look back at him and bite my lip as he let out moan after moan and declared his love for me. I knew this nigga didn't love me, just the way I gave him that pussy. I looked over at Sam and Tre noticing that they had worked themselves over and were ready to cum again. I opened my mouth to welcome them closer to me. One after another they came. Sam exploded into my open mouth. It wasn't a lot of cum, but enough to wet my now dry mouth. He tasted sweet as he poured the last drop on my lips allowing me to lick it off. At the sight of this Brian became even more excited and was slapping my ass as it shook on his hard-enlarged cock. I was licking the head of Sam's dick as he stroked, letting the pre cum cover my lips. I licked and toyed with Sam until he too exploded by letting out a grunt that resembled that of a victory cry after a battle. Brian, from all of the excitement and watching me drink from both Sam and Tre finally completed his quest as we both came hard and long.

All three men were exhausted as we lay there on the bed. I grabbed the blunt that was laying in the ashtray that was on the end dresser, lit it and passed it into the rotation. Before long the room was filled with the sweet high of purple haze. I lay there playing with my pussy as all three men watched until finally Sam opened my legs and began kissing my coochie with his tongue. My high had taken me as well as the deep strokes Sam's tongue was engaged in, that I had not heard the door open. Sam had stopped sucking my clit which caused me to open my eyes and question what was going on. I looked up to see Sleepy standing there watching. Tre' and Brian quickly grabbed their shit, got dressed and left. Sam didn't know what to do. He kept apologizing like Sleepy was my man or some shit. Sleepy just stood there mean muggin' them niggas. Sam had rushed out of the house and managed to slip going up the stairs. One thing for sure them niggas was shook.

"Damn, Sleepy, you sure know how to break up a party," I said wrapping my robe around me. Shit I was gettin ready for round two if you hadn't busted in and scared them, niggas," I said puffin on the blunt.

"Monica, you never cease to amaze me. I would hate to be on your bad side." Sleepy commented as he puffed the blunt that had been passed to him. "Did you get it?" He asked.

"Nigga I told you, this would be easy." I chimed in walking to the cabinet and unloading the camcorder that just captured my wicked performance with Tre', Sam and Brian. "Here, it's all yours." I confidently said as I handed him the tape.

"Damn ma. You know you didn't have to do this, we got people for this type of shit." Sleepy continued, looking impressed at my latest conquest.

"I know, but no one can do it like I can. Besides ain't nothing wrong with mixing business with pleasure. Them niggas think this was just a foursome, what they don't know is that, this little escapade is eventually going to cost them big." I added as I took another puff of the blunt.

"Remind me never to question your talents again. I ain't never seen three naked ass grown men move so fast!" Sleepy blurted out tryin' not to laugh.

"Yo that shit was funny as hell. They thought you were my man or at least someone that was about to bust on they asses!" I spoke laughing hard.

"So seriously, Mo, you sure that those three we need that's connected to Que and Jay's case" Sleepy questioned.

"Nigga, I told you I had this under control. Sam is the bailiff to the judge overseeing the case. Tre is the husband of the lead prosecutor on the case and Brian is the husband of the DEA agent that thinks she has a RICO connection to Que and Jay. That bitch is tryna make this murder case into a drug charge and criminal enterprise case. And we know good and damn well ain't nobody got shit on them'" I commented.

"And none of them knew each other?" Sleepy asked

"NOPE! That was the beauty of this plan. I could approach all of them separately seduce them and get them to come together for one night of nasty sex. See what happens when bitches don't suck a dick or get nasty for their husbands. That shit was too easy" I stated, taking my bow and my last puff of the blunt that was now almost gone.

"Damn Mo, you a heartless bitch" Sleepy added "They won't even know what hit them when all this shit goes down. Now we will have the inside connections. Que and Jay should be home in no time."

"We can hope so" I added

Just them my phone rang. It was Yazz. She asked if Sleepy was with me. I told her, yeah, and she laughed. "No not like that bitch" I replied. She gave me instructions to meet her at the house.

I jumped in the shower while Sleepy waited. I got dressed and we headed out the door. Sleepy drove as he headed out to Anika's crib. It sounded important and we also had news to share. Hopefully soon, Que and Jay would be out and free. Damn, I hope it was good news.

Chapter Eight
"Stay Cool" -The Roots

Anika

Yazz called and said the crew was on their way to my house. We finally got a reliable lead in Que and Jay's case. I had put money down on anyone who could deliver information aside from what Brenneman gave me. I needed information on the murder charge that was keeping my husband away from me and my sons, so I was willing to pay whatever the cost to get him home. So the streets were on notice. I made sure everyone knew the offer. Brenneman and I set up a tip line for information that ran directly into his law firm. At first, tips were coming in left and right. Most of the information was useless. I had paid for investigators to comb through the information and chase down leads. But as the weeks turned into months the information slowed down, hell it went from a fast-paced race to a slow ass crawl. So when Brenneman called, I arranged this meeting. He knew the business Que and I was in. Hell, he was probably the only one Que and I had clear and honest transparency with. Shiiid, Brenneman knew what color thongs I wore on any given day. That's just how much that nigga knew.

The doorbell rang. I knew it was Brenneman. If it was Yazz, Monica or Sleepy they would have used their keys or just walked in.

"Good, the rest of the crew isn't here yet" Brenneman stated as he rushed in the door with a serious look on his face.

Brenneman, what's going on?" I asked.

"Anika, we may finally have something. For months now the DA's office has kept shit on a tight leash. They aren't very forthcoming with the information behind this case. And with the trial date approaching, we needed a break. Well, we finally got one." He spoke while taking a seat and opening his briefcase.

"Well what is it" I jumped with a little excitement.

Just then the door opened. In walked Monica and Sleepy. They were joking with each other. It was good to see them getting along because lord knows it wasn't that way at first. The chemistry between them was almost a distraction to the information at hand.

Anna the housekeeper walked into the living room with drinks and some finger food. Sleepy sat on the love seat with Monica. Brenneman helped himself to the spread. I was trying to remain cool but knowing that there was information that could lead to Que coming home had my nerves in a pinch. I was ready to get on with this meeting. Not that I did not like seeing everyone, but I'd rather put an end to the bullshit so that life could get back to normal. And for me, that meant Que by my side. About 5 mins later Yazz walked through the doors carrying a Manilla envelope.

Anna closed the door to the office as we all set at the round mahogany table that had the numbers 716 carved in the center surrounded by the outline of western NY. It was a custom design Que had made. It was fitting as the FAM's operation started and was headquartered in the center of the area code 716. This small circle of power represented the heart of the family and my most trusted associates. I knew whatever was said and happened in these walls was as good as silent. I never had to worry about information spreading like bad gossip or feelings being hurt. It was business, and this was our top priority. Yazz went first. She opened the envelope and laid the contents on the table and began passing them around as she began to speak.

"So the informant goes by AP. One of the girls in the file room of the court building came across a document pertaining to the case. She is the girlfriend of one of the soldiers we have stationed on the block. She managed to get a copy of the document and gave it to Andre. I spoke with the young lady later. She promised to get me any information that crosses her path pertaining to the case. This is huge!" Anika finished with excitement.

"Anika, this could be the break we need. All we need to do now is figure out who the fuck AP is." Monica added.

"This could be any muthafucka, shiiid that could be initials, a nickname any fuckin' thing." Sleepy stated as he looked over the document.

They were right. It was good news, but the informant could be anyone. My head began to pound at the thought of trying to figure this puzzle out.

Brenneman chimed in after reviewing the document.

"AP is definitely initials, but whose is the question. Maybe this will help us," he paused as he opened his briefcase and handed the table a faint photo of an image.

"One of my private investigators camped outside the DA's office for 3 days. I instructed him not to move, but to account for every person he saw enter and exit the building over the course of 3 days. On the third day, we should be able to see who the regulars and visitors are. Everyone has predictable movements; we should be able to narrow things down. Well, this photo was taken at 10:30 pm on Wednesday. My investigator never saw him enter the building just exit. It wasn't too much out of the normal, except he was accompanied by the Assistant DA Brenda Kavanagh. It seemed important, so he took this shot right before he entered into an unmarked government car." Brenneman looked around the table for reactions, hopeful that this was another piece to the puzzle they were all working on.

Everyone shook their head in unison as all to agree that the photo was blurred and as far as they knew we were back to square one.

I was the last person to view the photo. My mouth flew open. It couldn't be. It wasn't. I shook my head and looked up at Brenneman. My expression must have set off alarms, because Monica asked, "What Anika, What do you see"?

I knew that facial profile. I knew the build of the person in the photo, I was a hundred percent sure. I had spent many nights looking at him from every angle. Blurred photo or not, I knew who the man in the photo.

"AP is short for Aaron Preston," I stated as I stood up and pointed to the picture.

"WHAT THE FUCK IS GOING ON!" I shouted as everyone reached for the picture again to take a closer look.

Chapter Nine

"Is That Your Chick"- Memphis Bleek

Yazz

After the meeting, Anika had pulled me to the side and delivered the message from Que. It was one thing for Anika to scold me, I would usually shrug off her relationship advice. She was wifed up with kids. Her obligations to Que were different than those I had for Jay. There was no ring, there was no written agreement. Just baggage. Just regrettable shituations that I could not take back and became harder for me to overlook. But when Que summoned me to do something, it wasn't an ask. I was being told and warned. Anika may run things on the outside, but Que ran things everywhere. Even though we were family, the fear of Que's reach scared me. I had seen the devil, rode for the devil, ate with him, l even killed for him enough to know when he tells you to do something, you obey.

I made my way to the prison. This time there was no backing away. My presence had been summoned. Besides, it was time. Que and Anika were right. I needed to be here for Jay. Even if I did not like to situation, it wasn't about me and my feelings. Shit falls apart when everyone ain't doing their part. Plus, I'm sure Jay was worried about me just as much as I was about him. Damn, deep down I just wanted things to be the way it used to be. No bars, orange jumpsuits and a dirty ass glass partition. I needed Jay by my side, not up, but right here with me. He was my calm. Without him next to me, there was no balance. I went from peace to pieces. And without balance, I was swaying more to the left than to my right.

    I walked into the heavy glass doors. I grabbed a number tab from the dispenser and waited to be called. I waited to hear them call for number 24. They were on number 98. I always tried to come before the mid-day count. But these muthafucka's was going so slow with the check-in process I may not make it. It had been a while since I had made an appearance in the waiting room. I did not want to tell Anika that I was coming. I did not need her judgmental eyes or tone of her voice pissing me off today. Plus I did not want my first visit in months to be a prison booty call. I just needed to see him, talk to him. I'm sure sex would come eventually, but I wanted that feeling like when we would go to the Delaware Park in the wee hours of the night and talk. I needed that. I needed him to hear me vent. I wanted to be his sounding board again. I wanted to feel the way I did when life for me was simple. Before I became consumed by this life. When the only thing I worried about was making sure Jay loved me and I loved him.

    I did make it a point to dress sexy though. I wanted to make sure that Jay knew I was still that chick he had at home. I was sexy but managed to still obey the dress code for visiting inmates. I wore a pair of dark denim tight jeans and a cute pink shirt. It was unbuttoned just enough to peak curiosity, but not enough for the guards to have a problem with it. The chain Jay gave me with our initials wrapped itself around my neck. I had on a pair of hot pink stilettos with white polka dots on them. I smelled of CK One which was one of Jay's favorite scents on me. Looking around the waiting room, we were evenly divided half women half men, but a light crowd for Wednesday. You could always tell who was here to see who. Moms always sat with a positive outlook. They dressed comfortably in sneakers as if they would be here for hours. Girlfriends always seemed to dress with a little something extra. Whether it was the lip gloss or the heels most could barely walk in, I'm sure the extra effort was appreciated by those on the inside. Dads and Homies rounded out the rest of the crowd. "Number 24" the heavy voice yelled out across the waiting room.

I walked over to the counter, gave my driver's license and began filling in my information. I had memorized Jay's inmate number by heart. It had become a staple of the many things I had committed to memory. As I finished up the sign-in process, the CO at the desk smiled and said lucky man, two in one day. I looked at him confused, but annoyed. I did not have time for games. My visit was long overdue. I was just happy to see Jay, but I would be even happier to leave this place.

First stop, through the neon puke color cage. It locks behind me as I enter. Shoes off, tongue out, mouth open, pockets emptied, body searched and a quick walk through the metal detectors all before I even enter the room where I'll wait for Jay. The female CO just smirked and said enjoy your visit. I wanted to check her, but it was best I keep my mouth closed before I end up in here with Jay.

Normally I would be seated and wait for Jay to be brought into the room. But I guess today was my lucky day. Not only was he already seated but he was not alone. I stood there watching him and some bitch having a friendly chat. It took him a few seconds to lock eyes with me. Yeah, nigga be surprised because apparently you weren't waiting for me to visit. Didn't look like he missed much of anything especially me. I pointed over to Jay so the babysitter of the visiting room knew who I was here to see. I walked over to the cozy couple and sat across from them. Jay stood to greet me with a puzzled look on his face. I would forgo the formalities for now. For now.

"Yazz this is Belinda, Belinda Yazz." Jay introduced us.

She smiled and said hello. I think from the look on my face she knew I wasn't one for small talk.

"Belinda, who the fuck are you?" I inserted into the small talk that Jay and Belinda had inserted me into.

"Yazz," Jay spoke in a concerned tone.

"No, it's ok Jay," Belinda spoke in a calm manner. I just came to visit an old friend. Wanted to make sure Jay was holding up good in here. You must know what I mean." Belinda continued looking me square in my eyes.

"Bitch! No, I don't know what you mean," I said raising my voice. This caused the correction officer that was stationed at the desk located in the visiting room to look up in our direction.

"Jay, I think it's best I leave. I'll see you next week." Belinda stated as she stood smiling at him and rolling her eyes at me.

"You should leave, staying would be bad for your health." I added as I looked her up and down.

Jay sat there speechless. Belinda left and it was him and I. Jay just sat there staring at me. The look in his eyes was nothing I was expecting. It was a cold absent stare. About five long minutes went by before I mustered up the courage to say anything.

"Who the fuck was that, Jay? Why did I even waste my time coming up here if you got other bitches to take my spot? Have you been fuckin with her all along? You trippin' nigga if you think Imma let you treat me like this." I spoke as I leaned forward in my seat pointing my finger in Jay's direction.

Jay sat there in silence. Hands folded. Eyes focused solely on me.

I sat there waiting for a response.

"So, what you don't have anything to say?" I questioned.

"It figures, you would pull some jail bullshit on me. I just can't believe…"

"YAZZ SHUT THE FUCK UP!" Jay yelled causing the whole room to become silent and focused on us.

I had never heard him speak to me in that tone or that way. I was scared and surprised.

Jay sat there in the dingy yellow chair looking at me. His calm demeanor was overturned by his now aggressive statue. I had noticed that the vain located at this temple was pronounced and carried the throbbing echo of his heartbeat. His jaw was clenched shut and his fist was balled up like he was ready for war.

Jay

I had come to love the visits from Belinda. I had forgotten how much I enjoyed our conversations. She always challenged my view on life and worldly events. Spending this short time with her brought back good times. Now don't get me wrong, Belinda was cute, fun and a good person. While we had never dated, she always held a special place in my heart. Besides when the only people coming to visit is your lawyer, Anika and Sleepy. Having someone not a part of this world I live in visit gave me normalcy. Belinda was one of the few people that could make me smile and laugh. Even behind these bars, she had managed to help me see the bright side of things.

It had me seeing her in a different light. One I never thought of before.

We sat there engaged in a deep conversation when all of a sudden the guard called my name.

"Jay, Visitor number two coming in." The CO commented.

Visitor number two. I wasn't expecting anyone, so I was surprised to see Yazz entering the common area. "What the fuck was she doing here" was my immediate response. But there was a piece of me that welcomed the sight of her. Even with all her attitude and her b-girl ways, she still made my heart skip a beat.

She walked over to where Belinda and I were seated. I could tell there was a problem by the look on her face. I could care less honestly. Belinda and I kept talking. Yazz sat there for a hot second before she began to show her ass. I tried introducing her to Belinda, but that did not go so well. I loved the thought of Yazz being a little jealous but her rudeness was annoying. And my patience was thin.

I sat there many of days wishing Yazz would pay me a visit. I missed her voice, the way she said my name and her smile. The Yazz that had shown up here today and over the course of my being locked up was someone I barely knew. I didn't like her tone or her negative energy. I was already surrounded by doom and gloom so the last thing I needed was her ass up in my face with this shit. She had managed to run Belinda off. The one person who has been a constant in my life these past months and this bitch got the nerve to be mad. I just sat there quiet. Shaking my head. Disappointed. And I wasn't even sure if I was mad at Yazz or myself. All I knew was this right here at this moment was not what I needed.

Yazz kept going, talking shit, like she had a right to know anything. Her voice irritated my soul. I wasn't one of those street niggas she gave orders too. So her tone and words fell on deaf ears. I sat there looking at her as patience wore thin. I watched her and my heart became sad. This isn't what I wanted. This can't be what I've waited months for. I held it in as long as I could, but 6 months of waiting, needing and loving a figment of my imagination burst out of me like the pain that my consequences have caused.

"YAZZ SHUT THE FUCK UP!" I yelled not caring that all eyes were now on us.

"I don't know who the fuck you think you are, coming in here and talking to me that this" I spoke as I grabbed her arm and pulled her closer to me. "I don't take orders from you EVER! I don't care if we in the streets or I'm stuck behind these bars, I am not one of them niggas off the street. You got me all fucked up. It's been six long months and you think you can just come up in here and act like I'm supposed to be excited to see yo ass? Like you not answering my calls or returning my letters is fine with me. What the fuck is wrong with you? Who the fuck are you?" I continued as I let my grasp on her arm go. I was looking into her eyes, the sadness that rain down, soften me on the inside. My exterior self would not cave in.

"I think you need to leave. I said as I got up to notify the guard that I was ready to go back to my cell.

"Jay wait" Yazz cried out.

I did not look back. It had been six long months without a word from Yazz. And today she showed up acting as if I owed her an explanation. I didn't owe her shit, she knew my situation, but me, I didn't have a clue about what she has been doing. No calls, letter or visits. And today I was fortunate to have her grace me with her presence. She can miss me with that bullshit. I had enough shit to worry about and was not going to add her drama to it. The door opened; the guard led me to the next checkpoint.

I took a quick look back. Yazz sat there with tears in her eyes as she watched me distance myself from her literally and figuratively.

Chapter Ten
"99 Problems"- Jay Z

Anika

So Aaron was back! What type of shit was he tryna pull? Is he really the reason why Que and Jay can't get out? What information could he possibly have on Que that the D.A. is using him as a witness against them? I had a thousand questions racing through my mind. How could he do something he knew would hurt me? Wait, I didn't really need an answer to the half question. Of course he would want to get back at me. But not like this. I needed to find him and put an end to this deadly game he was playing. But where was he hiding out at? That was the million-dollar question right now. I could only keep this information form Que for a short time. It was best that he hear it from me first. At least I could control the narrative and the actions that followed. I'm sure Que will not see it my way. I'm not even sure why I would be so lenient in my judgement of Aaron right now. None of that mattered if I didn't find him and put an end to this shit.

I put Monica and Sleepy to work. I knew that with the videotape Monica made, she would be able to use that to get some information. I knew that it was just a matter of time before we zeroed in on Aaron's location. And when we did, I would be the first person to have words with him. Yazz was already working her angles to see what other information she could get. A plan was in the works, well sort of, but it was enough for us to move. We were running out of time. Que and jay's trial was set to begin in a few weeks. I needed to stop this shit before it was too late. If Aaron was a key witness for the D.A., then it was my job to make sure he kept his mouth shut or I would shut it for him.

"You have a collect call from an inmate at The Erie County Correctional Facility. Quincy Thomas, to accept this call press one. Thank you for using Inmate Services powered by CTX. This call may be recorded or monitored." the auto system relayed the message as I hurried up to press one to be connected to Que.

"Hey Baby" Que spoke once we were connected. "Tell me something good" Que continued.

I was never good at keeping things from Que. I knew he could tell in my voice that something could be wrong.

"Hey, Papi" I greeted him with caution. I did not have enough information to fill him in yet, so I needed to play this cool. "Only good news is that I love you" I replied.

"How are my sons doing?" He added.

"Missing their Daddy." I chimed in. "They are growing up so fast, It's hard to believe they will be two years old soon. I'll have to send you some updated photos from us at the park last week. They look more and more like you every day. They even have your bad habits." I said jokingly.

"Bad habits, no such thing," Que said laughing. "My sons are perfect, just like their mother," he finished. "Anika, I don't know what I would do without you right now." Que spoke with a sudden sadness in his voice.

"Hey! Soon Baby, soon, I promise you, soon." I quickly rebuked the tone and thoughts that were creeping into Que's mind.

'I Know. It's just..." Que tried to finish his thoughts before I cut him off.

"There is nothing that will keep us apart. This is temporary. You know this Que. We will be back together before you know it. Don't lose sight of that. My love for you, our love for each other is stronger than those bars. This is temporary. And at the end of it all, I will be standing by your side." I stated

Que sighed, took a deep breath and spoke" So when a nigga gonna see you?" changing his tone.

"Damn, I can't surprise you," I said with a sly tone.

"You know a nigga don't like surprises Ma. I need to see you" he replied.

"I'll be there tomorrow." I acknowledged.

"Kool thanks shorty. Tomorrow it is. I know I don't even need to tell you. Same time?" he questioned.

"Same time baby, and no you don't even need to ask. Sexy just how my nigga like it" I said smiling as tears rolled down my face.

"Anika.," Que spoke

"Yes, Que.." I answered

"No tears Ma. No tears. Let me do all the worrying. You stay strong and handle the business and take care of my sons. You told me soon. Then soon it will be. No Tears!" He commanded. "Anika.."

"Yes, Que.." I answered

"I've loved you since day one, and I love you more now than I did then. I put that on everything I know and have, believe that. I'll see you tomorrow lady. One love. Que finished.

"One Love" I repeated

"Thank you for using Inmate Services powered by CTX." the automated system chimed in as we ended the call.

I had to find Aaron and fast. I don't know how many more calls like that my heart could take. I needed to get Que home. Him and Jay. Aaron, I'm gonna find you and when I do, you better pray I can undo the mess you've caused. You better pray I have mercy on your soul.

Chapter Eleven

"Snitches' - Master P / Snoop Dogg

Aaron

"Yeah, mommi suck that dick," I said standing there as her lips caressed my swollen manhood. I had her hair wrapped around my hand like I was styling her hair. I held it with such force that it guided her head up and down my shaft at the pace I needed to get off. I rammed her head up and down, up and down until I exploded deep into her throat, letting out a grunt that mimicked the sound of a warrior.

Toni was cute. She was the Assistant District Attorney that I met when I put this plan into place. Not only did she fall for the dick, but she believed every word of my story. Hell, the parts of the story I couldn't make up her ambition and overactive imagination filled in the blanks. She was gullible, to say the least, and if it wasn't for this plan of mine and her throat game, I would have never approached her. Toni's eagerness was a complete turn-off. I liked girls that I can chase. That played hard to get. The minute I stepped foot in her office she was ready to drop the panties. And the fact that she was married told me all I needed to know. Her loyalty was only as good as the opportunity in front of her. She could not be trusted. And once Que and Jay were locked behind bars for good, Anika would have no choice but to come running back to me. The sooner this trail was over the sooner I could get my life back.

I would leave Toni's office later tonight night as I had done for weeks now. It was always after dark, I was always picked up and dropped off. The District Attorney's office felt that it was best I be protected until the trial got underway. So I played along. I don't know what they thought would happen to me especially since Que and Jay were being held in the County Jail without bail. They didn't even want me out and about until after the trial was over and Que was locked up on all the charges my story brought about.

I have to admit; this shit was too funny. Who would have thought a chance conversation I overheard at a bar one night would lead to me getting the girl of my dreams back? Anika didn't know it yet, but everything I was doing was for her. She deserved better than that hood street nigga Que. She needed someone who could love her right, someone who could give her the life she needed, provide the things she wanted. Hell, I am even willing to take on his bastard kids and give them a proper home, even give them my last name. By the time I'm done with Que, I will have erased him from memory. My plan is working so far. That nigga has been locked up for over a year now. All I have to do is stick to the story and of course, keep fucking the Assistant D.A. Soon Anika would be back in my arms.

Who would have thought that night at the bar, overhearing a conversation would give me enough ammunition to take down the one person that stood in my way of happiness? I heard enough information to put the rest of the story together. They never said who killed the young man, other than it was some wannabe drug dealer. They gave just enough information as they chatted over Hennessy. There were two things I knew for a fact, niggas drinking Hennessey leads to loose lips and stiff dicks. These two niggas were gone. By the time I joined the conversation they were so relaxed, I didn't even have to ask any questions they just gave me the information. I had details and dates and enough information to make the story my own. By the end of the night, I had come up with a plan to take back my life and the woman I loved. I sobered up and went home and started to put the plan into motion. By the time I'm done, Que would wish he had never met me that day for drinks. I often think of that day, like he gave me permission to have Anika. Did he really think I was going to just give her back to him without a fight? He may have won that day in the hospital, she could even marry him, but just like that, it could all be taken away. And that's just what I was going to do. Take everything Que loved and make it mine.

Yeah, that nigga Que is about to get everything he deserved. By the time I was done, he won't be the king of anything but a jail cell. I thought to myself as Toni started rubbing and caressing my back. Before I knew what happened, she had already kneeled at my feet with her mouth open welcoming my dick into her warm mouth. This shit was too easy. Her ambition and drive blinded her from seeing everything I was using her for. Toni was no Anika, but she'll do for now, besides a dick getting suck doesn't need a name, face or loyalty, it just needs two lips and a warm mouth. Toni's warm mouth will do. Ohhh yeah, Toni's dumb ass will do!

Chapter Twelve
"My Neck, My Back" – Khai

Monica

Tre' was so excited that I had agreed to meet with him and his wife. The last time was the night of the foursome. The thought of his tongue rolling and twisting between my thighs made me wet. I met him at his home address. Which meant I drove all the way to Niagara Falls to get my pussy licked. I had to remember that this was a twofer, yeah my carnal desires were going to be taken care of, but this was also an opportunity to get the Assistant D.A. on film. This was something we could use as leverage in getting to Aaron, and ultimately getting Que and Jay out from behind bars.

Tre' had a tongue that was made for licking pussy. The dick was good too, but the way he sucked and fingered me had me on edge. His face was deep into my pussy. The hairs of his goat-tee tickled my thighs as I arched back and allowed my juices to spray him in the mouth. He had one finger in my ass, one in my pussy, and his lips suctioned to my clit all working in unison as my body shook and convulsed from the pleasure of him playing me like a musician plays his instrument. He held me tight in the grip of one arm while strumming my insides to the beat of my throbbing clit. He was a master at making me cum, the way he spit on my pussy and then dove back in to lick it up. I lay there on the kitchen countertop of the home he shared with his wife allowing him to contaminate his holy matrimony in the most unholy of ways and it turned me on!

Tre's dick hit all the right spots as I bounced up and down on it. He gripped my ass and joined in the race to the finish line. His dick remained hard no matter which way I mounted him. I went from slow glides as my ass cheeks stroked him into quite moans to fast and hard strokes as I fucked him laying on top of him. I rode as long as he stayed hard. We fucked and fucked until our bodies were dripping in sweat. His fingers tried grippin' my body but the moistness of my body allowed only for temporary holds and fingerprints left on my body. He held me tight as I made my way to the home stretch. I could feel his dick twitching which indicated that he was ready. I unmounted my ride and dropped to my knees in one move to catch the reward of a ride well done.

We were just finishing up when we heard the garage door open. Perfect timing I thought. I was sure the house smelled of pussy the way Tre and I had been going at it. We had just finished getting dressed as the door opened. In walked his wife. I knew it was her from the photos that adorned the house. I could tell from the look on her face that she knew what we had done. And that was fine by me. In her mind, we had gotten the party started without her. Little did she know this encounter would be the gift that keeps giving.

"Baby, you're home," Tre said rushing to his wife's side. He planted a kiss on her cheek with the same lips that bathed in my pussy.

She grinned. "Hello, you must be Monica. Tre told me about you, but he never mentioned how pretty you were." She stated looking me over.

I had almost forgotten that this was supposed to be a threesome. Tre had told me his wife was into women. She would sometimes allow him to bring a girl home for both of them to fuck. I could tell by the look on her face that she approved of me in every way.

She walked around me admiring my curves and phat ass.

"See baby, I told you I knew what you liked." Tre' said proudly as his wife's smile agreed with what her husband said. Tre' had managed to pour us some drinks as the Assistant D. A. introduced herself.

"Please sit and make yourself comfortable. My name is Antoinette, but you can call me Toni," she insisted.

"Hello Toni, I'm Monica." I replied taking the glass of wine from Tre'. "You have a beautiful home," I replied.

"Thank you," Toni said looking around admiring her decorative skills.

She had managed to move closer to me on the couch. By this time the wine was flowing and the small talk became more flirtatious as Toni played in my hair and her hand rested on my thigh. I noticed that Tre' conveniently had left the room and disappeared. I guess Toni was feeling brave, she had taken a hold of my hand and led me down the stairs and into a room in the basement. The room was all black. There was a king-size poster bed that was wrapped in black satin sheets and a matching comforter. Tre' had already removed his clothes as he sat on the bed waiting for us. The confidence these two displayed told me they were pros at this game. But when it came to sex, I was a master. I just hoped Toni was up to the challenge and could lick and suck as good as her husband.

I made sure to bring my purse with me. The small camcorder sat nestled in the purse which was resting on the dresser that was located on the South wall facing the bed. It was still on record from when Tre' and I got started earlier. Oh, it had been capturing all the festivities even Mrs. Assistant D.A.'s flirtatious behavior on the couch. It was time for the main event to begin and with both of them rubbing on me, my body was ready to perform.

Toni wasted no time finding her way between my legs as her soft lips caressed my inner thighs and her fingers fondled my breast. I stood there facing both of them Toni kneeling at my feet and Tre' seated on the posted bed stroking his dick. I could hear the soothing tones of music playing in the background. I was relaxed as Tre's lips sucked and caressed my breast. Toni's tongue had found its home as she tasted my juices. I had grabbed her long brunette hair and forced her further into my pussy, as I lifted my leg so that she could really enjoy me. Tre' was now kneeling in front of me on the bed. He was at the perfect height for me to suck his dick. Toni's sucking set the pace at which we all moved. I had Tre's dick in my mouth working him with one hand and controlling his wife as she devoured my pussy with the other. As if in unison Toni joined me as we both begin to suck and stroke Tre' dick. Together we each took a side of his shaft and loved it until it was long, stiff and ready. Without a word, Tre' pulled me onto him as I continued the where we left off earlier that day. I rode him like a stallion. I took his thick long dick into me. Stride for stride we fucked in perfect rhythm. Toni tried to join in, but Tre' had made it very clear that he was sharing me. It left her only option for joining in to sit on his face. By his reaction, it wasn't something he enjoyed at least not the way he had enjoyed me in that manner. Toni rode Tre's tongue trying to match the strides of my gallops on his dick. Tre's moan of approval brought about looks of disappointment from Toni. I could tell that by the look on her face Tre's reactions to my movements and body were things she had not been able to achieve in their marriage. Maybe this was the first time Tre' had brought home someone he wanted to fuck verse someone she wanted.

Maybe this was the first time Tre' set aside his desire to fulfil his wife's needs and selfishly satisfy his own wants. Whatever the reason, Toni's jealousy was starting to show on her face.

I could tell that Tre' was deep in the zone. His strokes were deliberate, with every touch he excited my scenes. The way we grinded against each other and enjoyed the passionate kisses we blessed each other with was like shots of sunshine on a cold winters day. There was an organic, sensual connection being made in the middle of what should have been a group encounter. It turned into one man's journey of either revenge or self-gratification. Either way, I was along for the ride.

We finished our tryst by engaging in a hot shower where we all joined in. It wasn't long before the sensual touches led to instant foreplay with tongues, lips and hands leading us into another round of marital sexcapades. After we were finally done, I thanked both Tre' and Toni for the experience and their hospitality. Something tells me that they would long be talking about me. That was about to be truer than they both thought. I'm sure Toni would not want to see me again, but thanks to my little camcorder, she and Tre would see me a lot sooner than later and this time licking my pussy would be the least of their concern.

Chapter Thirteen

"Oh Boy"- Cam'Ron

Sleepy

I made my way up to county. I made a point to get up there weekly. Que and Jay was family. Ain't no way I was gonna have them be locked up without me making an appearance. Besides, I was where I was because of these dudes. Wasn't nothing to me, shiiid doing a bid was like a badge of honor, sort of like how my man Mario went out in a blaze of glory. That's the shit legends are made of. They needed to know that I had their back especially since Que had wifed up my cousin and had little shorties out here. Unc Sleepy was on the lookout. These dudes didn't have to worry. I had their backs, fronts and all that in between. It was all love. Like I said these niggas was my boys, and we had each other, I was just doing what was expected amongst family.

I made my way into the cage after being pat-down and the walked through the metal detectors. Que and Jay were both there already. We dabbed each other up. I quickly gathered some snacks from the vending machine, copped some drinks and grabbed the dominos from the community table. It did not matter where we were at it was always like old times. We had mad jokes going. I had to clown Jay. Monica had shared with me Yazz's drama.

"Jay, say it ain't so? Both your bitches show up on the same day. How the fuck you do that? Don't tell me you been up in here that long that you gettin' your days messed up!" I laughed taking a sip of the cold Pepsi from the vending machine.

Que burst out laughing "Yo he came back to the unit hot as hell. This nigga tell me what happen and I died. I told him he better be happy Yazz wasn't strapped, that'll been his ass" Que barely got out without laughing.

I stood up and started swinging at the air to mimic Cuba Gooding Jr. in Boyz In The Hood. "Yo Que was he in the block getting it in like this?" I continued laughing hard. Que and I laughed until tears rolled down our faces. Jay sat there taking it like a "G".

"Y'all niggas think that shit funny. That bitch was wrong, all the way wrong for how she came in there like she did. I had to go hard on her". Jay paused. "That shit was mad funny, Yazz on a whole nother level. That bitch was about to beat the fuck out of Belinda. Belinda didn't want none of what Yazz had. Hell, I was proud and pissed at the same time" Jay laughed.

"When Monica told me that shit I died yo, dead ass died" I chimed in dabbin' up Jay.

"I didn't think he had it in him, Sleepy. Jay been soft since day one for Yazz. Yo, their first fight happens when he locked up and can't fight back. This nigga just got up and walked out. Said visitin' hours is Ova!" Que fell over laughing. We all joined in laughing.

"Fuck Yall," Jay said jokingly.

"Seriously," Que changed up the conversation, "How's business?" he questioned.

"Que, business is good. No scratch, that business is boomin'. Anika handling shit like a pro. The shit she got us into is making more money than anything we did in the past. Everyone respects her lead, Mommi doin' her thing. You should be proud." I answered Que with honesty.

"How is Yazz handling her responsibilities?" Jay asked.

"Yo you saw how she burst up in here! I said jokingly". "No really Ma is smart. She thinks now before she acts. Anika stays on her, but I think that just a sister thing. She makes sure everything is everything. From everyone in the territory, they got mad respect for the ladies and how they handle business. We sitting good, the only piece of the puzzle missing is yall two niggas." I stated while grabbing some Cheetos out the over-priced bag from the vending machine.

'So, how far are we from figuring shit out"? Que asked as he searched my eyes to make sure I was stating facts.

"On some real shit, Imma let Anika fill you both in. We on to something, but she knows more than me right now and that's how it should be. If you want answers, Anika will be your source." I spoke making sure I looked Que in his eyes. He wanted answers and even though we were boyz, rule number one in The FAM was loyalty to the throne and right now Anika sat on top. Que knew that and I knew he would respect me for following suit.

'You right" Que commented and nodded in approval of my decision not to give out info.

"So, not to change the subject, but how are things going with you and Monica"? Jay said with a smile on his face.

"You got jokes now nigga," I said shaking my head and laughing.

Que started laughing, "He ain't ready for Monica's ass!" Que commented shaking his head.

"Yall nigga's tryna clown me. Ain't nobody scared of Monica's ass." I piped up and disclosed.

"So you hit that shit?" Jay asked.

There was a slight pause on my part.

"Naw that nigga didn't hit that shit" Que laughed chiming in.

They both started laughing. "Hold up jailbirds. Naw I didn't but it doesn't mean I don't want to. First, that was Mario's girl, I don't do leftovers. Second, she still not over him, I'm not wit messin' up chicks heads like that. Third… Damn that bitch badd!" I said breaking down and laughing.

"Nigga I knew you were lying, since when you pass up pussy"? Jay spoke

"Word!" Que said. "Unless Monica isn't feeling you?" he continued.

"Both of yall can go to hell! That bitch been throwing that shit at me since day one. But it's bidness, you feel me. Bidness and bidness only" I said laughing "But Damn that bitch badd, I ain't even gonna front I can see why Mario was tryna wife her up."

"Ain't either of you try hollering at her," I asked leaning in.

"Nigga NO!" Que said firmly. "I can peep trouble a mile away and Monica smells, looks and sounds like trouble with a capital T" he finished.

"'So you trynna tell me she ain't bad" I questioned.

"Naw Nigga neither one of us did that. What we know is she ain't the wifey material.

Besides if I ever fucked with Monica, I would have never ended up with the women of my dreams. But I had to put them blockers on cause that body be on point. She a badd bitch." Que admitted

I knew that shit was honest, what Que just said because Anika was the finest thing I had ever seen and she was my cousin. So if Monica caught Que's eyes and it was difficult for him to not look, shit now they knew how I was feeling.

"Every day is temptation island with that chick", I said shaking my head.

"For real though, you and Yazz, yall gonna be good"? I asked

Jay sat there for a minute before answering. "I'm not sure anymore," he spoke with pain in his eyes.

Que and I just looked at each other.

"Nigga enough off all the emotional shit. Let's finish this game of bones so I can take a yall candy. Que yelled out, "Dominos Niggas!".

We played another round, ate some more junk food from the vending machine. I caught them up on all the latest shit from the streets. I would do it all again next week. We were family, and if it were me, I would want these two niggas to have my back.

Chapter Fouteen

"Da Baddest Bitch"- Trina

Anika

My dad told me a long time ago, telling a lie was like living in a four-wall room. It didn't matter the size of the room or the size of the lie. "The goal was to make sure you cover all angles of the lie or room to make sure the lie stood. You can't live in a room without a floor and a roof. Much like that room, your lie has to have a strong foundation and enough cover to block out any unforeseen elements, your floor and roof. Once you have the foundation laid and you've looked ahead enough to cover the unforeseen, you need to make sure your story makes sense. The walls hold up the roof and are secured by the foundation. All walls need to come together to protect you, protect the lie. If one wall falls then so does your protection, hence the lie crumbles." I remember my conversations with my dad now more than ever. His knowledge of the streets, the hustle and relationships help steer me clear in my new position. Hell, I didn't even realize just how much I had paid attention to the shit he told me until I found myself peepin' game, handling business and trying to understand how to stay five steps ahead and look ten steps behind me to make sure my moves stay solid and undetected. "Finally," my dad would say " Make sure those angles are 90 degrees at all times. Those angles be your accomplices, events, or anything or one you bring into your lie. They need to be stand up stand witchu kinda niggas. They make the walls stronger and unbreakable. They reaffirm your story. Your lie becomes their truth. Don't bring anyone into your lie or room, your house you can't trust with your life. If they not down for you the way you down for them then leave them niggas and bitches on the outside of your room or life. If not, the room is only as good as the angles holding up the walls and the roof. If they too wide the roof will not cover you, leaving a hole in your life or lie. If they come in too close and they leave the foundation exposed to the elements. Thus, damaging how and what you stand for both in life and within the lie." he finished his analogy. His goal in telling me this was simply don't lie, but what it taught me was how to be better at it and how to detect one. Something I had neglected to do with Aaron.

It would be this same reasoning I would use to untangle this web of lies Aaron must have told to cause all this drama in my life. I thought that day in the hospital I made it clear to him that it was over. I hoped that he leave peacefully. After all, I have pictures of him and his alternate life. Evidence that could destroy his professional football career. Something I hoped never to use or bring back up. Aaron was forcing my hand and now that I knew he was behind the reason why Que and Jay were being held, the reason my sons have gone without their father, I would use that information and anything thing else in my arsenal to bring him down.

I had gotten the tapes from Monica. I had arranged a little impromptu meeting with my special guest. It was time to put an end to this bullshit and bring my husband home. Sleepy was taking care of some business for me. The boys were with the nanny. I was on my way to see Que. On my last visit, I had brought him up to speed on all the information that had come to light. Brenneman had his private investigator still scoping out the federal building. He was hoping we could tail the car that Aaron was in and find out where he was hiding out at. Even if we didn't get a hit, I was confident that the plan I had in place would work.

I made my way to the county jail. Made my way through the formalities for visiting an inmate. Today I didn't even mind the extra groping offered by the Corrections Officer, who obviously didn't know who I was or who I was coming to visit. Que had made it very clear to the guards at the facility that I was off-limits. They were being paid very well to do what Que needed them to do. Everything from extra time at the mess hall, private rooms for him and I to talk, allowing him and Jay to be able to live as much like home as possible. Within these walls he was King and that carried over into the streets. Being his wife gave me leverage. I had instant respect just because I was his. And even within The FAM, niggas followed me out of loyalty to Que. Yeah, I sat on the throne and controlled things, but niggas were especially careful not to cross any lines for fear of Que's reach. It extended far beyond the walls of his cell.

I had made a career out of juggling my family responsibilities and those of The FAM. I had even managed to keep up my duties as a wife. Just because Que was behind bars did not mean that I could let myself go. My body was boomin more so now than ever before. Having the twins pushed my hips out just enough to even out my ass and breast. I was a full-size Coke A Cola bottle. My curves aligned in all the right places. I kept my hair and nails done and no matter where I went I was dressed like Que was by my side. So when I step inside the prison I was dressed to impress my man. I could care less who else was looking and drooling. My priority was Que and giving him something he could feel, see and imagine when I wasn't there.

I was escorted into our personal room. It didn't even bother me that while I undressed, the two correction officers that escorted me to the room stood there and watched. They knew better than to do anything but look. It wasn't long before the door opened and in walked Que. He dabbed up the correction officers as they exited the room and we heard the door lock behind them. I stood there in a pretty hot pink and brown bra and thong lace and satin set. I kept my brown stilettos on, which gave my ass the pop it needed as the slight arch in my back help my pose as Que stood there looking me over.

" So now you giving the Co's a show," he said jokingly as he walked over to get a closer look.

"They just casualties of this war Pa," I coyly replied.

"Damn Anika, we don't even stand a chance! Now me and them gonna have hard dicks up in here." Que confirmed.

"I can't do much about that problem for them, but I definitely can help you with that," I confidently said as I grabbed ahold of his bulging dick imprint. I rubbed it as I pulled him closer to me. His hands searched my body and his lips covered my neck as he planted passionate kisses. As if a choreographed dance I had Que undressed and leaning against the table. I squatted down in from of him and blew on his dick as it raised to attention.

"Oh, how I've missed you," I whispered as I took him into my wet mouth.

He tasted so good. I had missed the way I made his dick grow inside my mouth, I could get him to a full erection as I stroked his dick up and down. I held his balls in the palm of my hands as I wet his shaft so that my spit dripped down onto them allowing me to massage them as I sucked on him. Que's knees shook with approval as I worked my way up and down back and forth along his now fully erect dick. He moaned and held my hair in his hands as I glided up and down. I held onto his thighs as my nails dug into him forcing him even deeper down my throat. I didn't gag, I just inhaled as if I was taking in air and allowed him to penetrate my air passage. I felt him squirt warm liquid deep down my throat. He tasted just like I had remembered. I drank all of it as Que stood there looking at me in awe. I stood up as Que grabbed me and tongued me down. It was a long hard kiss that required no pause. I was pressed deep into his chest. Our heartbeats joined in unison. His manhood still erect and swollen, was begging to enter me as it jumped against my leg.

Que picked me up and slid my thong to the side. Holding me as if I was light as a feather, my legs wrapped around him as he entered me. I rode him and rode him as he jammed his hard cock into me. His hands pressed into my back as I held myself up going up and down on his dick. Que braced himself as I fucked him hard and long. He held me tight and I moaned in his ear. My arms wrapped tight around his neck, I bucked and bucked and bucked until I could not take it anymore. I fed him my breast as I climaxed all over him. Que bit down softly on my nipple as I screamed out in pure satisfaction. He sucked on me like my beast belonged to him, like he craved the milk that they produced. I continued to ride him, my legs wrapped and knotted behind his back. He gripped my ass and assisted with me bouncing up and down on his shaft. We went fast and then slow. We went hard then soft. With each motion I went all in. I gave him strokes for each day since my last visit. I kissed him for every minute we had been apart. I fucked him craving his seamen to enter me and seed my womb.

"Oh, how I've missed you," I whispered in Que's ear.

"You missed this dick baby," Que grunted.

"I miss that dick baby. I miss how you make mommy cum on that dick," I screamed out in pleasure.

"Daddy knows mommy, daddy knows," Que whispered. "Cum for daddy baby, Cum for me," Que begged.

"Yes baby, yeass!", I replied, giving way to all my senses that had been heightened from his massive dick stroking the walls that lined my enter sanctuary. "Yes, daddy, Yess!", I grunted

"Give it to me, Anika, give me what I want baby" Que begged as he fucked me even harder.

I bucked back and gripped his back as the sweat from our bodies colliding leaving me slipping and losing my grip. I bucked and he smacked my ass. Que pulled my hair back exposing my neck to his aggressive kisses. He pumped and I bucked and together with the slapping of our bodies against each other I released all of the stress and worry onto Que. He, in turn, gave me all the power and courage to continue as needed. It was a fair trade-off. It was what was expected as husband and wife. This was the for better and worse that we each willingly signed up for. It was what we needed when we needed it. It was the marriage agreement unspoken.

Que carried my limp body in his arms over to the chair as he rested with me laying in his arms. We sat in silence. I could hear his heartbeat drum a soft low tone. It was what I missed most about sleeping alone. I slept on Que every night. It was my safety blanket, listening to his heartbeat. Being in his arms gave me a sense of peace and calm. This is what I would do anything for. To have this right here back in my life, I would sell my soul and kill for this.

There was no interruption as Que and I took our time dressing. We went over the plan I was working on. Que didn't say a thing. He just nodded with approval. I did not leave any details out. It was well thought out and I had covered every angle and scenario. I think I made my father and Que proud at that moment. Que smiled as he held my hand. I wished that I could capture these moments to take with me to our sons.

Que had given me some things to take care of for him. I sat on his lap facing him looking into his eyes as he asked me about a few business-related things. I could tell that he was on board with my plan because he didn't even ask for me to review it with him again. His eyes told me that he was ok. Not just with the plan but with us, with life. He wasn't worried. He knew I had his back. He knew I was about this life and that no one or thing was going to stand in the way of our happiness. Not even Aaron.

We sat there talking about everything, from the boys to me and anything else he wanted to know. I shared the milestones that he was missing out on and filled him in on everything he had to look forward to when he got home. He kissed and held me and for a short moment, I forgot that we were situated between cinder blocks and iron bar. We had spent 3 hours on this visit and yet it seemed like just a few minutes. I needed to get going. I had to get back to my reality. The boys needed me and business never sleeps. Most importantly I was ready to go hunting. With Que's approval, I was ready to hunt down and take care of the one thing that was standing between me and my happiness. Aaron would pay for his actions. I was going hunting, my goal was blood, and the trophy was reuniting my husband with his family.

Chapter Fifteen

"U Should've Known" Monica

Yazz

The hunt was on. Anika had confirmed the identity of the informant was Aaron. I knew that nigga was a no-good asshole. His snitchin' ass was in for a showdown. Everyone was on the lookout for him. It wouldn't be long before we had eyes on his whereabouts and then it was all up to Anika. And for his sake, he better pray I don't see him first. I shoot and ask questions later. My gun has a bullet with his name on it and I guarantee I won't miss that target.

It was all I could think about finding Aaron and that bitch Jay up there visiting him. Between the two, one of them deserved what they got, the other deserved worse. I guess it was going to depend on who crossed my path first and what day it was. I drove around the city handling business. It was about 6 p.m., the evening rush hour traffic had just let up. I was in need of a drink and I knew there was a happy hour happening somewhere downtown. I promised myself that I would stop at the first sight of a bar. This proved more difficult than I thought since most of the streets off of Main Street in the downtown area were mostly one-way streets. I made it to the intersection of Seneca Street and Washington Street. I sat in the truck facing the Buffalo Bison Baseball field patiently awaiting the light to turn green. There off to the left. Perfect, a little hole in the wall tavern. And since there wasn't a baseball game tonight, it shouldn't be crowded. Lowkey is what I needed. That and a couple of double shots. I parked the car and walked in.

The bar was sparsely lit with just as many patrons. I sat at the bar waiting. I had the bartender keep the double shots of whiskey flowing. I sat there watching the faces of those entertained by the static infused ball game that was playing on the dated TV in the corner of the room. There were faces that showed their age, faces that hide secrets and faces that searched for answers but only came up with empty bottles of sorrow. It was a place that only those in silent pain frequented. And I fit right in. It had been almost an hour of me sipping and thinking before Reggie walked in.

Reggie had a lead on Aaron. I asked him to meet me here. I called him from the payphone located right outside the bar as I walked in. Reggie was a police officer The FAM had on their payroll. Reggie was smooth and easy on the eyes. We flirted with each other many times back in the day, before Jay.

"I'll have what the lady is having" Reggie motioned to the bartender.

"What do you have for me Reggie," I asked getting right to the point.

"Slow down, momma. I'll give you what you want. Can I at least enjoy my drink first?" Reggie said sarcastically.

"Reggie, don't get it twisted, this was no social call. It's business." I stated firmly.

"It's always business with you. You're too young and beautiful to be so serious." Reggie commented. I could feel his eyes looking me over. It was almost as if he knew. It had been months since I felt Jay's touch. It had been months since it even felt like we were in a relationship. I began to think it was showing on my face. No one in their right mind would press up to me knowing Jay was my man. Either he knew or didn't care and wasn't scared of the consequences.

We sat there finishing up our shots. I tried to remain hard in my composure. But sitting there and occasionally making eye contact with Reggie, something was brewing inside of me. And I needed release. I wasn't sure if it was the liquor talking or my emotions, either way, it was coming out.

We took the last sip of whiskey. Reggie took my hand and led me to the back of the bar. Without hesitation, I followed. He pulled me in closer to him and our lips locked as we rushed into the men's bathroom stall. Without a second thought, I had unzipped Reggie's jeans and cuffed his penis in my hands. It was hard and massive. I could feel his dick throbbing in my hand. He wanted me and I needed him. My mouth watered at the thought of having him. I could feel my panties getting wet as he caressed my breast. His hands slid down my jeans and into my panties. His fingers stroked my clit as I rode them in anticipations for the arrival of his dick. With one hand he unbuttoned my Levi's 504 jeans pulling them down enough to release one leg as he lifted me into the air and buried his face between my thighs. His tongue had awakened me like the warm sun as my juices flowed out of me onto his lips. I held his head as he licked and savored me. As he loosened his grip on me, and gently placed me on his lap as I straddled him and began to ride him. I picked up my speed as we both bucked and grinded. Tears fell as I relinquished control and gave way to my selfish desires. As I moaned, Reggie grunted. And before we knew it we had both climaxed. Without saying a word. It had begun and ended.

Reggie and I slowly made our way out of the restroom. He was holding my hand just as he did leading me in there. He stopped abruptly, making a clearing in the hallway for me to see. There before my eyes was Aaron. He was leaving. Reggie covered my mouth as I began to scream out his name. Reggie held me back. I tried to loosen his grip, but I couldn't break away. Aaron was right in front of me and had couldn't do anything about it.

"This is what I wanted to tell you all along, Aaron comes here every week, same day and time for a drink." Today is not the day you want to do this. You need to be smart about this. One wrong move and that nigga gonna run. You need him alive and you need to capture him without the emotions Yazz. You and your team will get him but not today shorty. But next time you'll be ready. Next time he won't have anywhere to run to and nowhere to hide" Reggie whispered in my ear.

As mad as I was at Reggie for not allowing me to chase after him, he was right. Now I knew where he would be and next time I would be ready. We would be ready. Aaron was on borrowed time. I could not wait to tell Anika and the rest of the gang. Soon all of this would be over. One way or the other Aaron was going down and Jay and Que would be coming home.

Chapter Sixteen

"Bring Em Out" -T.I.

Anika

I didn't have time to go to the jail and talk to Que. Things were happening so fast since Yazz told us where we could find Aaron. It had been four days since she told us and we were already putting a plan in place. I had visited the bar that Aaron frequented. I had a long persuasive conversation with the owner. He agreed to allow us to staff the bar for the rest of the week. We had people positioned in and around the bar for intel. I wanted to know the coming and goings of everyone that entered or worked around the bar. I needed names, addresses, habits, favorite drinks, work schedules and anything else they could come up with. I wanted no stone unturned. If I was going to take Aaron down I needed to make sure he was acting alone and if there were others, I wanted them too. Plus, Aaron was smart enough to carry out this plan so far, I knew he would be smart enough to see me coming. I had to be careful and our plan needs to cover every angle if it was going to work. I wanted this bastard bad and there was no way we were going to fuck this up.

Sleepy had rented office space directly across the street from the bar. He did surveillance from that location. He had been watching all those in the area. He had eyes on everyone and everything that went on in that block. By day three he could tell me the habits of everyone. What time some took cigarette breaks, left work or who was late for work and what office romances took place. Sleepy's main goal was to let me know the coming and going of everyone that patronized the bar. I wanted to see if there was any connection to Aaron. And if we were going to make a move we needed to find out this shit now. We didn't have the time to play this safe. We were already two years behind and with the trail set to start soon, we needed to get to Aaron and end this.

Sleepy gave me a report daily. He did not miss anything. He was one observant muthafucka. He caught any and everything that looked out of place. There was a log of license plate numbers that he called into one of the officers that worked for The FAM. This spot was a haven for some of western New York's grimiest white-collar criminals. With the information we gathered, you would think we were working with the Feds. I was amazed that we stumbled upon this. But when you think about it, I shouldn't be. Buffalo has always been known for its ties to the Mafia and the Underworld. Once Sleepy told me this information, I had to make sure that we were on neutral territory. The last thing I wanted to do was start a war with the Italians or some other clan going after this nigga. All I knew was there was some connection to Aaron and this Bar, but what. And the fact that all the elite of the white criminal world seems to make an appearance here made me concerned. I was concerned but not enough to stop the plan. If there was an issue with what I had planned, I would handle it after the fact. Priority one was getting Aaron. But I could not shake the feeling I was missing something.

Wednesday had rolled around faster than a crackhead's lip could wrap around that pipe for the next hit. I stayed away from the area. I did not want to take the chance that Aaron saw me. I could try to play it off as a coincidence, but Aaron would know better. He knew me enough to know

I was up to something. I stayed in the Fruitbelt at one of the stash houses waiting for the call. It was still early in the day. But we were all ready. Sleepy and his crew had the block covered. There was no way Aaron was getting away today. The minutes on the clock went by slow as fuck. Patience had never been a trait of mine and it showed especially today. I kept a cool head even though on the inside I was a ball of fire. I could not wait to get my hands on this fool. Everything he had done to me, my sons and Que, and for what, because he lost, because Que married me, because of the twins? There were too many scenarios that made no sense to why he would do this to me. When I said goodbye to him in the hospital that day, I thought he would walk away gracefully. But no, this nigga wanna be extra. He must have forgot what information I had on him. And he certainly had underestimated me. He would soon find out.

It was showtime. Reggie and the bartender confirmed that Aaron usually comes in about 6:00 p.m. It was always as the crowd dwindled down. Aaron sat in the back booth and ordered the same drink. Rum and Coke. He was so predictable. Everyone was in place. Sleepy had me on a burner phone giving me blow by blow coverage as if he was the commentator at a sporting event. Everything was going as planned until Sleepy paused. It was a long pause as if he knew something was wrong. Just then the phone dropped and I could hear the scattered steps of feet running out the door and Sleepy yelling "WHAT THE FUCK"!

Chapter Seventeen

"Don't Say Nuthin'" - The Roots

Sleepy

"WHAT THE FUCK!" I had drooped the phone as we all ran out of the office and down the flight of stairs. I can't believe this shit.

"Which way did he go?' I yelled out. As half of us ran left and the other half ran right. Anika's perfect plan had one major flaw…Yazz.

"Yo, what the fuck kid" I directed to Yazz. What the fuck you doing here? I continued shaking my head as I placed my hands-on top of my head.

"You just fucked everything up. Anika is going to be pissed, you crazy bitch." I warned.

"I was just trying to do what no one else would have done. Yall wanna talk to that Fagot, I wanna put a bullet in him." Yazz walked up to Sleepy with her gun at her side.

"If you don't get that shit outta my face, I swear I will choke the shit out of you". I spoke as our eyes locked. Yazz was three seconds away from me laying my hands on her. Up until this moment I had never had a reason to hit a woman. My mother raised me with at least that much knowledge. Even with me living this lifestyle and all the crackheads and triflin' bitches I came across not once had my emotions moved me to lay hands, but this reckless bitch had me on ahunnit.

"YOU STUPID BITCH" one of my boys screamed out.

"Who the fuck you calling a bitch"? Yazz cocked her gun and pointed at his head.

"Yo Yazz"! I said with a stern voice. "Yo beef ain't with him." I continued as I stepped in between both of them. We locked eyes once more.

"Did anyone see where that muthafucka went? Anybody see any goddam thing!" I yelled out. There was a sea of silence that waved across the crowd. Just then Brandon and Mookie returned. They had managed to chase Aaron down an alley. He got away, but not before they were able to get a partial license plate and the color and model of the car. My headache tensed, and my fist wanted retribution for the carelessness that had occurred. But nothing prepared me for Anika pulling up.

"Please tell me that you accidentally shot that muthafucka," Anika demanded as she exited the truck she drove and pulled up onto the curb where we were at congregating.

"Awe Shit," I whispered to myself.

"Tell me the reason why Sleepy dropped the phone and I drove over here like a bat out of hell is because yall beat Aarons ass and got him tied up in the bar waiting for me? Please tell me I'm right." Anika clapped her hands demanding an answer.

She was mad as fuck and so was I. There was no way I could clean this shit up.

"SOMEBODY BETTER SAY SOMETHING BEFORE I GET TO BUCKIN'! Anika yelled out.

"Anika, It was me. I underestimated Aaron. He hesitated to enter the bar. Almost like he knew something was wrong. I saw him about to make a run for it. I jetted out after him and tried to catch him but I, we, couldn't catch him." I spoke up looking at Anika and focusing my stare at Yazz.

"BULLSHIT!" Anika yelled out. You want me to believe that the most meticulous muthafucka I know just could not cross the T and dot the I?" Anika paused.

I could tell she was pissed. Ever since we were kids whenever Anika couldn't get her way or she was mad, or when she cried, her nostrils would flare up. Well, she wasn't cryin' but she didn't get her way, plus she was mad, so you can imagine the steady breaths and the flaring of her nostrils was something that would scare most people, especially those that had not known this side of her.

"You wanna know what I think? I think You covering for someone. And the only thing stopping me from pulling out my gun is that we blood. Only thing I know is that Aaron's ass is still out here, and my husband is still locked up. If you got a weak link on this team you better get rid of him. You better fix this shit Sleepy. Or I will forget that we share the same blood and treat you like a nigga that just lied to my face. FIX THIS SHIT! I WANT AARON BY THE END OF THE WEEK AND Y'ALL MUTHARFUCKAS BETTER DELIVER," she concluded.

"FUCK!!" Anika screamed out loud as she walked back to the truck, hopped in and drove away.

Everyone stood there in disbelief. I stood my ground, looking at Yazz. She had fucked up big and I knew Anika would have had Yazz's ass for dinner. I could take it. Besides, all bullshit aside, she knew I had her back. Yazz's recent actions had placed a strain on Anika and her relationship. A girl fight right now would not be in everyone's best interest. Anika was right though; we had a weak link and I needed to handle it. Yazz walks up to me as if she wanted to say something.

"Bitch you owe me one," I stated grinding my teeth as I walked in the opposite direction leaving her standing there like the fool she just played.

Chapter Eighteen
"True Love" - Faith Evan

Anika

I drove around frustrated, angry and mad at the world. "WHY" I screamed at the top of my lungs. It was all I could do to hold back the tears. Drove to the only place I could think. I sat there in the parking lot with my head down trying to figure out what happened. I knew that Sleepy was lying to me. But why, what went wrong? How could Aaron have escaped? Why was he doing this to me? All this and more tore at my soul. It broke down the barriers and walls that I had built up over the past two years. My tough exterior was crumbling, and I needed to be with the one person who saw past all that hard exterior and allowed me to be vulnerable. I had called ahead as I had done so many times before to announce my arrival. I pulled myself together enough to make my way through the steel doors of the back entrance of the officers' gate. I wore my pretty girl face on the outside, the one the world wanted to see, while on the inside the absence of innocence I had lost so long ago gave way to tears as she cried for me.

I made it past the guard station and was escorted into one of the many private rooms Que and I have reserved. It was the one time that I loved the fact that this lifestyle afforded me privileges normal people couldn't have in these situations. It provided comfort in a time when most had scared glass visiting stations or congested visiting areas filled with unwelcoming eyes and cold stares. In moments like this I needed Que most. And as much as I wanted to hold it down for him, I was losing it. I was walking in steps he was only meant to occupy. I had adapted to the lifestyle for love and he was born to the life out of necessity. We were polar opposites and without each other we were useless, but together we were electrifying. We were power, love and destruction. A force, both good and bad.

I saw him standing there, he turned to face me as the door opened. I ran to him and wrapped my arms tight around him and cried. He held me. No words, just the sound of our hearts beating. The tears rolled down my face at a steady pace. I closed my eyes and imagined that I had come to tell him he was coming home. That I was successful in getting to Aaron and he confessed to the lie and all charges were being dropped. That the twins were ready to see their daddy, as I watched him hold them again in his arms as he had done almost two years ago. I wished it had been the way I imagined. I wished this was the last time I had entered those gates and the last time I had to recite his inmate number 962864. I was ready for the nightmare to end. I was tired of the tough girl act. I just wanted to be Anika, Que's wife, mother to our sons. I needed him free. I needed us free. Free.

"Anika baby, what's wrong?" Que questioned.

I could not bring myself to tell him I failed. He grasped my chin gently and lifted it.

"You're my queen. There is never a reason for you to hold your head low. There is nothing you can do that we can't fix baby," he spoke in a calm soothing tone. "So tell me why you're crying. Are the boys ok?" He pulled away to make sure he could see my response.

"The boys are fine." I replied.

"Then what's wrong lady," he questioned me gazing into my eyes.

"I tried to go after Aaron, I had a lead and I acted on it. I was so close... But he got away." I confessed as tears rolled down my face. I had tried to pull away from Que in frustration. But he grabbed my hand and kept me within arm's length.

Que gently wiped the tears off my face and held me in his arms. "Anika." He paused waiting for me to respond. "Anika," he broke his hold on me and lifted my head so he could look into my eyes. "Anika, this isn't your battle baby. Thank you for trying to go after that nigga, but you have to trust me when I tell you I'm going to get out of here." He spoke with confidence.

"I know, but I was so close.." I tried to explain before Que cut me off.

"Anika, do you know why I love you?" Que asked still looking me in my eyes.

I stood there shaking my head as if to say yes.

"Anika, I love you not because of your looks, or your body. You're fine as hell, but just being attracted to things that are superficial would be a bad thing to build a strong foundation on. It was your heart. I fell in love with your giving soul, your kindness, the naive way you look at the world. You made me want to be a better person, you made me believe that I deserved love and that I was capable of loving. You showed me a world I had never thought was possible. So I worry that the woman I fell in love with, the mother of my sons is trying to be something she is not. You can pretend out there if this is what you need to do to be ok while I'm in here. But the one place you don't have to pretend is with me. I need you to be soft, naive and full of hope. Because if you lose that I would never forgive myself. You're not in this by yourself. I'm here. We're in this together Ma. I'll take care of Aaron. His beef ain't with you, it's me he's after. I'll take care of his punk ass. Do you hear me?" Que concluded.

Our eyes locked and at that moment I believed him. I knew he would be home soon in my arms and all this shit with Aaron would be over. I shook my head once more as if to say yes. Que held me in silence. At the moment, nothing else mattered. I could be me. No Gangster, not the head of the notorious FAM, just me, Que's wife. And he let me be just that. This is what I wanted all along and this was how things were supposed to be. He held me in the dark cold cinder block room. This had felt more like home than my address and it was because I shared it with Que. His heart was my home.

He held me until the tears stopped. With just his touch Que made everything whole again. I knew what had to come next and I knew I had to let Que handle it. Whatever he needed me to do I'd do it. If we were going to get him and Jay out of here, I had to let the king of the street deal with Aaron. Aaron better pray for forgiveness, because all hell was about to break loose. Even from behind bars, Que's reach was limitless and now that he knew who was behind him being where he was, Aaron's days were numbered.

Chapter Nineteen

"Ante Up (Remix)"- M.O.P feat Busta Rhymes, Tephlon and Remy Ma

Que

"I don't know what the fuck is going on out there, but I know one thing, if I see my shorty again with tears in her eyes all you niggas gonna pay. I promise you muthafuckas that shit." I spoke with certainty as my jaw tightened. I had gathered the heads of all the territories for a meeting at the jail. This included Jay, Yazz and Sleepy. Monica was finishing up an assignment I need completed ASAP. It seemed like she was the only one handling business when it came to that nigga Aaron. I didn't say how she was handling it, just that it was getting done. And if Monica did everything right, Jay and I would at least be out on bail by the end of the week. This way I could finish this shit once and for all with Aaron prior to the trail.

"Do you niggas hear me? Am I clear on this?" I asserted as they all looked me in my eyes searching for the bluff.

They all vocalized in unison, "Yes"

"We're done for now", I announced. "Jay and Yazz I need to see you both before you leave". The door that was guarded by the CO had closed as all the members of The Fam existed the secure room we were using as a conference room.

I stood facing Jay and Yazz. There was silence. But I could see on their faces that they both had plenty to say. But no one's mouth dare open.

"Ok, fuck this! Yall two need to say something. Either work this shit out or walk away, but what we not about to do is let yall relationship fuck up business." I stated breaking the ice.

Yazz rolled her eyes and Jay huffed.

"Nigga, is that your bitch?" I questioned Jay. There was silence.

"Yazz is that your nigga?" I questioned again Yazz looked away.

"Fuck Yall! Don't answer me. I get it none of my business. But I tell you what, let me hear how you fuck something else up again Yazz and I personally bring it to you. And Jay, if you not in her corner then cut loose nigga. Yall fucking up the flow of business. And when you fuck up my money then there's a serious problem. Fix this shit one way or the other but yall not leaving until it's fixed." I said slamming the chair against the wall. "I'm out. I got shit to do" I stated walking out of the room frustrated.

I had made my way up to the cell. I couldn't help but think of Anika. All that I had asked of her, I just couldn't sit here anymore. It wasn't so much the throne, it was knowing that what I asked of her, needed from her was way more than I wanted her to handle. She was cut different from me. She graduated college and I was a student of the streets. She was cultured and I wasn't, and when it came to being grimy, her hands didn't need to get dirty, that was my position, and I had made it difficult to play that role in my current state. Soon, that would all change if Monica could deliver. It was time for me to get the soldiers ready, better yet it was time to shut this shit show down once and for all. Aaron had played his hand. This nigga collected a few books, but now my hand is trump tight and it was time I slapped them shits down for the win.

Chapter Twenty

"Are You Still in Love with Me"- Keith Washington

Jay

I stood there trying to figure out what to say. Words with Yazz had never been difficult to come by. There were so many things that had happened between us and for every good thing in our relationship there were about two unrepairable actions that I could not mend. I stood there looking at the monster I had created. I wanted so bad to love her and keep her for my own. In the process, I had damaged the one thing that I treasured the most. The distance between us only added to the issues that neither one of us wanted to face. The silence confirmed how I was feeling. Normally we would be all over each other buy now. I haven't felt her touch in so long, I wasn't even sure if deserved to anymore. Hell, Que was right, we had let this interfere with business. I was willing to at least put our personal feelings aside for the sake of business. If there was anything left to savage of our relationship, we could handle it outside of these concrete walls. Maybe by then, it will work itself out one way or the other.

Yazz

I don't even know where to begin. I can't even look at him right now. There's a piece of me that wants to run to him. Have him hold me and erase the past couple of years. Take me back to a time when I didn't know what it was like to pull a trigga, a place where I had not known bloodshed and my hands weren't dirty and my soul was clean. I remember long walks in Delaware Park and nights where the only thing that mattered was his embrace. I wanted that back. But I'm not sure if we can. The person Jay fell in love with is so far gone, I'm not even sure if I know how to get her back. I tried and the guilt won't let me. Not to mention the other bitch he had up here. That was the last time I even saw him. He hasn't called and even if he did, I'm not sure I would have answered. There were just so many things that have happen. I wasn't sure if we can overcome them or if I truly wanted too. I could feel the tears forming in my eyes. I could not allow myself to cry. I wasn't sure if they were tears of sorrow or remorse. Would I even cry at the loss of us or for the freedom that came from the constant reminder of all that went wrong in the relationship? I needed more time. I just couldn't make that decision right now. Que was right I needed to handle business. I needed to stay focused on the task at hand. Jay and I was a distraction right now. I just couldn't bring myself to say the words, not now. Not like this.

"Yazz" "Jay" we both uttered at the same time.

It was the first time either of us smiled in the 45 minuets that we had been in each other's presence. It was an awkward familiar interaction.

"Yazz, you go first" Jay spoke.

"I was just going to say…" I paused.

"I know." Jay paused.

It was a conversation neither of us wanted to have. It was a necessity. One that would stop the heartache and pain or bring on a new beginning or maybe both.

"Why don't we just agree to focus on business for now" Jay stated in an melancholy tone.

"Jay, I agree. We need to handle business right now. There will be time …" I tried to complete my thoughts but before I could Jay grabbed me and kissed me. The warmth of is lips, the heat from his well chisel body instantly took me to a place I had distant memories of. It was the familiar touch I had missed and longed for. I wanted more, I wanted him to wash my insecurities away and wanted to submit to him, become the woman he wanted me to be. The girl he looked at and made feel like she was the only one in the room, the one he fell in love with. But when I opened my eyes to say the words to express my feelings, all I saw was Jay's back side as he walked out the doors that had held us hostage.

Chapter Twenty-One
"B K Anthem." – Foxy Brown

Monica

"All I could do was laugh. You should have seen their faces." I said gloating about my latest mischief. "So, let me finish telling you what happened," I continued.

"I had shown up to the District Attorney's office. I told the receptionist that I had an appointment to meet with Toni Richardson the ADA. After looking me up and down, she escorted me to the waiting area. Toni came in just minutes after me. She was looking all professional and shit. It was hard to look at her without thinking of how her lips and tongue had caressed my pussy on our last encounter. In fact, her and Tre' fought over who could lick me better as they battled for control over my body. I could tell from the look on her face I was not the person she was hoping to see. I'd imagined it had something to do with me using a fictious name.

With a side eye she escorted me back to her office. It was a very masculine office. It reminded me of something off of the show Law and Order. Something some pompous white man decorated in all custom wood shit and the walls were lined with books. It smelled like money, power and bullshit. Toni did not seem amused at all. Her whole demeanor changed once we were behind closed doors.

"What are you doing here?" she asked abruptly.

I had an appointment with you. Seems we have more in common than you know." I responded.

"I'm afraid we don't have anything in common. I'm not sure what hole in the wall bar my husband found you at, but you can go crawl back there and stay." She commented as she leaned back in her oversized chair.

"Naw Ma, we got more in common and you might want to find out what that is before you dismiss me like some cheap whore. In fact let me show you a little something. I took the envelope I was carrying, opened it and pulled the disk out the case and placed it into the Television set that was located on the south wall of her office. I grabbed the remote and hit play.

Within minutes Toni, Tre' and I appeared on the screen.

"Wow, Toni! You definitely know how to perform for the camera." I commented as sounds of sex echoed throughout her office. I turned the volume up as she ran over to the television set and manually turned it off.

"How did you...?" Toni said with a horrified look on her face.

"Don't worry about the how, all you need to know is I have copies and I'm ready to broadcast this show. Your coworkers might like to see your Oscar winning performance. Let me ask you something, what would happen if they knew their little token black girl was a dirty ass whore? Do you think that tongue of yours would make it to District Attorney with the election being right around the corner? I mean I'd vote for you, you nasty bitch" I laughed out loud.

"Shut the fuck up! Shut up!" she screamed as she charged at me.

I grabbed her by her hair, bringing her to her knees. Toni had come out of those Manolos as she fell, done. I held her hair pulling her head back so I could make sure she had a clear view of what I was saying. There were tears in her eyes, that reminded me of a time when I was trusting of everyone. But those tears would fall on their own, I didn't have a tissue or a fuck to give.

"Listen closely to me Toni, that video remains a secrete only if you cooperate. I need to know where I can find Aaron Preston?" I questioned.

I don't know an Aaron…"

"Bitch don't play me!" I spoke yanking her head back even harder. "You know who the fuck I'm talking about. I need a number and location. Because this little case you trying to put together has made a lot of people antsy. You're making more enemies than friends and in a year for elections we can certainly make things happen. Things that lead to you having the career you always wanted, or we can end you. Have your ass making the 11 o'clock news and not because you won shit." I aggressively warned her.

The look on her face said she was both intrigued and scared.

"Good, now that I have your attention. Delivering Aaron is just part of what I need. I need you to let Quincy and Jason out."

I could tell by the look on her face, she knew what I was talking about.

"I just can't do that. How would I ever deliver my star witness? Everyone will suspect something now. We are so close to the trail." She stated shaking her head no.

"That's not my problem, what I do know is that YOU will make it happen. Besides you're a very talented women, I'm sure you will figure it out." I said letting my grip loosen on her hair.

"I just can't." Toni said as tears rolled down her face. "What about my career? How can I do something that goes against everything I stand for?" Toni uttered

"You will or your private life becomes very public. And trust you me, we've got you on tape with about a dozen women, you and your husband. Now you wouldn't want to tarnish that good girl image by not doing what I asked." I said smiling a devious grin.

Toni sat there on the floor of her office. For such as strong driven hard woman, she had shown her vulnerable side to me yet again. It made her look weak to me. Almost like she lived for the limelight, but was actually a scared child, afraid that her deep dark secrets would be found out.

"TONI!" I screamed, "snap out of it. There is only one way out of this. Drop the case and give up Aaron's location. I promise you my friends will be grateful for your services".

"How do I know you're not lying? How do I know I can trust you?" Toni's spoke looking up at me.

"You don't. All I can say is you'll have to do your part and then everything else will fall into place. Besides you have everything to lose and everything to gain, if you play your cards right." I said as I opened the door to Tony's office.

"Girl for crying out loud, fix yourself, get off the floor, you've got work today. Remember I need results, I'll call you later." I said closing the door behind me.

Chapter Twenty-Two

"Get it Poppin"- Joe Budden

Sleepy

While Monica was busy handlin' chickie, I was busy handlin' the men. Monica had set up a rendezvous with Tre, Brian and Sam. It was time they pay up. Monica's performance with these niggas was enough to make anyone blush. It was time they see just how famous Monica was about to make them. As soon as the doorbell rang, one by one they entered the house. I watched from the other room as they each shook hands and made themselves comfortable. I guess they each had several things in common. From what I've heard an encounter with Monica was a coveted prize. Being that these niggas had been lucky enough to have her at the same time must have felt like winning the lottery.

I waited a few minutes making sure they were comfortable enough that my presence would not send them running. I heard one of them ask where Monica was at? The other chimed in and said the text said she'd be here shortly. That was my cue. I walked into the livingroom with my gun by myside. I was hoping not to have to use it. I just wanted to scare the muthafucka's a tad, enough that they wouldn't try anything funny.

"Good evening fellas" I spoke upon entering the room. I could tell they were startled. The look on their faces told me they remembered me from the last encounter with Monica. There was silence.

Well hello to you too, Bitchassniggas" I said laughing." Monica will be joining us shortly. I called this meeting because I think it's time we get to know each other…"

"I thought Monica asked us here?" Tre questioned as he rudely interrupted me. The other two shook their heads in unison.

"Nigga if you ever interrupt me when I'm talking it will be the last words you speak. Like I was saying, I have a little situation, that requires your cooperation. I'm hoping that we can resolve the matter quickly and without incident." I continued as if I was never interrupted.

"What can we possibly assist you with?" Brian said in a very sarcastic manner.

I'm glad you asked Brian. You're married to DEA Agent Tabitha Collins, right?" I questioned. "You live over off Maryvale Road and Transit. Two daughters, Kimberly and Janice?" I questioned him again. I wasn't looking for an answer, I just needed him to know I knew who the fuck he was.

Brian gestured as if he wanted to hop off the couch and attack me. "Not so fast nigga. You might want to sit your ass there and be still." I waved my gun giving fair notice.

"You better not do anything to my family" Brian cried out.

"Don't worry, all is good if you play your part."

Brian was shocked. I could tell the other two knew if I had this much info on Brian, I had just as much information on them.

Sam asked" What do you want from us?"

"It's simple." I stated. "I need yall to convince your wives to stop the trail of Quincy Thomas and Jason Burd."

"And why would we do that?" Tre defensively asked.

"Because if you don't Tre' I'm going to put a bullet right between your eyes. Since I can't kill your wife you'll have to do nigga. And if Brian here doesn't do his part, those pretty little girls of his will become turned out bitches on some corner in some town wishing that I had put a bullet to their heads. Not only will I destroy your wives careers, but I have enough dirty on all yall to make the devil apologize. Oh yeah, you all have secrets, and if you don't cooperate everyone will know just what the fuck you've been hiding" I said as I sat back in the chair and hit play on the cd player.

They watched their sexual encounter with Monica as it played. Live and in living color. The pleasure shown on their faces as they collectively dishonored their wedding vows and gave way to lustful sin now met with disgust and anguish as they watched themselves. But that was not all. I played clip after clip of all their little secrets and that of their wives. It appears it was enough to make one blush or at least repent for their sins from the look of horror on their faces. Sex with other men, sex with minors, taking bribes, and doing drugs. Hell, it made what I do look like child's play.

Just then Monica opened the door and walked in. She could tell by the silence in the room that the cat was out of the bag. There was no excitement in their eyes, No one was naked and waiting. All she could do was laugh. "I see you started without me" she proclaimed. Well at least we can cut to the chase. Tre' I just left your wife; I can tell you she wasn't happy to see me either. When you get home, the two of you may want to have a long talk. Brian, a copy of all your indiscretions and your wife's secret drug addicted escapades was sent to her office today. I'm sure she will come to her senses too. And Sam, you've been a dirty boy. Playing the file both ways. Being that you're still in the closet and want to stay that way, it's in your best interest to take me up on this offer. I would hate to go public with all this information. I'm sure that's not what you want. Oh and whatever he said too" Monica continued as she pointed in my direction.

"I want the charges dropped by end of week. That's more than enough time don't you think?" Monica spoke as she took a sip of the drink she poured from the bar. All three guys sat there in disbelief. They had been played and now it was time to cash in.

Chapter Twenty-Three
"Breathe"- Fabulous

Que

I heard the gate lock behind me. The CO had walked me to the changing room. There was a package there for me. Inside was a new pair of jeans, a black long sleeve t-shirt, a new black leather jacket that still had the price tag attached and a crispy pair of white and black Air Force Ones. The CO handed me the folded brown bag that held the remnants of the items that I rolled up in here with. The only thing I wanted was my wedding ring and my necklace. The rest of that shit they could continue to fight over. Besides, I had never been one to flip over my clothes. I had enough shit in the closet and what I did not have I could buy. They could keep that outdated gear. I was ready to wash the last two years off and that included whatever baggage I came in here with.

Luckily for them my wedding ring and chain were still in the bag. I knew niggas knew better. Only a fool would test my patience like that. And after my stay in here, I have none. I got dressed and waited for the door to open. The CO dabbed me up and walked me through another set of doors. I heard the lock slam closed behind me. I walked the blocks one last time as all the soldiers gave me a final nod of approval. I stared straight ahead. They knew it was time for business. The look on my face said it all. It was war time and I had business to handle. There were shout-outs and cheers, mainly from niggas that had no clue, but my real niggas knew the walk, the game and my story. I wasn't much of a talker, but I walked the walk and talk the talk. My silence was everything. It spoke volumes about the type of player I was. Very few knew my moves and those that did, walked the same paths I did. They were trusted, tried and true. So, this exit, while planned was low key. Only a handful of individuals knew what was happening today. Anika was not one of them. I needed to protect her from what was about to happen next. I had one agenda… Aaron. I walked past the last cell and through the series of gates. Each one closing behind me. It was so final. Only a fool would think I would return. Hell, my first time was trumped up charges. There was no way I would be so careless. But now I was on the radar, and I would be kidding myself if I thought the Fed's found out more on me than they needed to know. Just knowing I existed was an issue, and now they knew my name. Everything from this point onward had to be done with precaution and executed to perfection. No loose ends and no bitchassness.

I walked through the last set of doors and was bathed in sunlight and fresh country air.

OOOOHHHHWWWEEEE!! I let out a cry.

It felt good. I walked toward freedom. And then smiled. I should have known; this nigga would be ready. Like peas in a fuckin' pod; like twins; we rolled tighter than fat bitches spandex.

Chapter Twenty-Four
"Illy"- T.I

Jay

I knew something was up. The CO opened the door and escorted me to another cell. It was temporary he said. "Temporary for what" I asked. He did not reply. What was even more disturbing, Que didn't even flinch. Now since day one of us being here, Que and I have been inseparable. In fact, The FAM had paid good money to keep us comfortable while we were here. Not that we would have beef with any of these niggas, nor were we scared. We had handled plenty of bitch ass muthafuckas before, besides most of the dudes up in here were down with us. And those that weren't wanted to be down with us. But the look on Que's face told me all I needed to know. That nigga was up to something. And the fact that he did not let me in on the secret could only mean that it was big shit.

Ever since we were kids, anytime Que had a plan, he would get quiet, almost studious. I could tell he was thinking of a master plan. And when he shut all the way down, it meant the plan was already in action. So, I went along with the CO. I nodded at Que and watched the sinister grin rise across his face. Whatever Que had planned, I was down. That's just how me and my Brother rolled. I had his back and he damn sure had mine. I walked down the hallway before being led into a side room. Inside the room was a bench with a brown paper bag. Inside was clothing. New clothing all my size. I heard the CO say, hurry up and get dressed. I knocked on the door when I was done. The co opened the door and we walked down a dimly lit hallway. I was handed a manila envelope as the guard opened the last door. The sunlight beamed down on me like I was under the spotlight.

I looked back at the guard confused. "What the fuck" I said out loud.

He just laughed and smiled. I was free. I was free from the iron bars and the shared space that I had called home for almost two years. The sun heated my soul as I stood there trying to understand what was happening. I took in the fresh air and it hit me. That muthafucka did it; Que managed to get us out. That nigga had more balls than anyone I knew. He was a true OG. I don't even need to know how or why; I just celebrated the fact that I was standing outside of the prison instead of in it. I tore open the envelope. Inside was a pair of keys and a note. The keys belonged to a car. The question was which one. The note had an address on it. I walked down the service road. Not hurrying my stride, but shit a nigga was free and I did not want to stand there just in case they decide to take my black ass back in.

I made my way to the front of the prison. I hit the alarm button on the keys, and it set off the alarm of a black Jaguar. Damn! I knew we would roll out of this bitch in style, but this was some other shit. The car was smooth. I checked out the glove compartment. It looks like there was everything we needed to handle business. Now I just needed to know the next step. I pulled out of the parking lot and headed back toward the service driveway I had just left. I parked the car there and waited. I was hoping my intuition was right. I got out of the car and posted up against it. I had nothing but time. I knew whatever was about to happen was real talk. We were street niggas. Business needed to be handled. I'm sure Que had an agenda. Without a doubt we were getting ready to cause some havoc. Someone had to pay for this shit we just went through. Niggas needed to be dealt with. Oh yeah, I was ready for some action. I had shit to do and an itchy finger. It had been almost two years that I sat my ass in that cell, over some bullshit charges. Oh yeah, ya boy was ready. The streets were calling, and I was ready to answer.

About thirty minutes later the same side door opened. I heard the steel door close tightly and lock. I saw a familiar image coming toward me. The walk at confidence. The stride said don't fuck with me. And the expression on his face said it was time to handle business. Just as I suspected. My nigga, my ace, Que had been freed as well. I heard him let out a roar. The lion was free to roam. And with me by his side, no one was safe. Que had a plan, and we would execute it to a "T". Yeah, ya' boy was free, The King was out, and together we were ready to roam the jungle and reclaim our fame. Long live The FAM! I cheered as Que appeared and we dabbed each other up. Que took on long look at the building that had divided us from those we loved and the streets we owned. He opened the passenger side door and got in. I followed suit. We drove off headed in the direction of Buffalo.

We had three long hours ahead of us. It was just enough time for Que to fill me in on the plan. Something told me the first stop when we got to the city was the address that was written on the note; 54 Sussex. Something told me whatever we were looking for we would find all the answer there. And right now, the agenda had one name on it, Aaron. Aaron had to be dealt with. And from the look on Ques face, that nigga did not stand a chance. Oh yeah, ya boy was free. The King was loose, and havoc was about to fall on the city of Buffalo, and I was down for all this shit.

Chapter Twenty-Five

"ATF"- DMX

Aaron

Shit! The other day I thought for sure that Yazz was going to kill me. But there was no way she knew anything about my current situation. Maybe she was just still mad at me from two years ago and what happen between Anika and I. Whatever the reason, I got the fuck out of there quick. Yazz was crazy. There was no need for me to pretend that she wouldn't try something. The look on her face said it all. And I just did not need that kind of drama in my life right now. I had moves to make and shit to do. The trial was fast approaching, and I could not wait to sit across from that nigga Que and see the look on his face.

"What the fuck you mean she's not available?" I asked calling into Toni's office. Ever since we started this investigation and she was able to arrest Que and his bitch Jay, Toni always made herself available to me. Hell, I laid the dick so good, she even made herself available to me when she was with her husband. "Fuck it!" I continued, "I'll just come down there." I told the receptionist on the phone as I hung up. It was weird. How dare she not take my call. I'll have to dick her down when I see her. Make her remember just how important I am to her case. Better yet, I'll throw this dick down her throat and make her gag as she slobs me down. That'll remind her. I thought laughing to myself as I made the drive to her office that was located downtown.

I arrived at her office building. I parked like I had done so many times before. If Toni didn't send a car to pick me up, I would either drive my Benz into town or catch a cab. I had a pass to park in the government lot. I'll have to check with her as to why the pass did not work today. I know this shit has been taking a while, maybe they expire after some time. Good thing the security guard knew me, or else I would be parking out in clear view. I knew how important it was for me to keep a low profile. Last thing I wanted was to be seen coming into the county building. I wouldn't want anyone to think I was a snitch. Hell, the only thing I was trying to do was fuck over Que and get Anika back. If anyone saw me, they could easily confuse the two.

'What the fuck dude, you've seen me many times before. Now I need to get up to the fifteenth floor. Stop playing and let me pass." I cried out loud to the guard posted at the front desk.

"Mr. Preston, I'm sorry but you're no longer on the approved visitor list." The guard commented.

"What the fuck you mean I'm not on the approved visitor list? You better get ADA Toni LaCosta on the phone. Don't you know I'm part of a major federal case? Once this all gets straightened out, I'll make sure that you lose your job!" I ranted.

The security guard just sat there calm and collected as he attempted to call up the District Attorney's office. After a long pause and a brief conversation with someone, he hung up the phone.

'Well?" I questioned looking for approval to continue my journey upstairs.

Within a matter of seconds the elevator doors opened, and out walked ADA Toni LaCosta.

"Finally!" I said out loud. "It's about time." I commented annoyed.

"Thank you Peter, I'll take it from here," Toni stated. She walked over toward me. I attempted to meet her halfway before she extended her hand to signal me to stop.

"Look, Aaron, we did everything we could, but the case was dismissed. We no longer need your assistance." She uttered.

"Wait a god-damn minute, what are you saying?" I questioned. "I can give you more information, hell I give you whatever you need. I'll say whatever you want me to, but we just can't let that muthafucka get away with this. Que must pay for everything he did to me... I mean what he did. How can this happen. What the fuck didn't you do?" I continued to question.

"Look here Aaron, the case was dropped. The information you provided wasn't enough to make the charges stick. Plus, some of the story and timeline you provided couldn't be corroborated. The defense has witnesses that are willing to testify and tear down your story. It just isn't going to work" Toni spoke.

"You dumb bitch, we knew that when I came to you with this bull shit story. Your job was to make it stick remember. You wanted this conviction so bad. You needed it to make your career. I recall distinctly that you wanted me to tell you more, hell, you even helped fill in the gaps. That was in between you sucking on my big dick. Don't you remember? I yelled out in frustration.

Toni grabbed my arm and ushered me into a corner.

"Listen here, It's over. You hear me? Over. If you come here again, I'll have you arrested." Toni warned.

"Bitch did you forget, I can ruin you. You orchestrated this phony story and plot to take them wanna be drug dealers off the street just as much as I did. I'm sure your boss would be interested in hearing what I have to say, or maybe your husband will want to know about all those late-night sessions we had." I counter warned staring her up and down as if to say checkmate bitch.

Toni laughed, "You better run. You better not pass go. You better run like you got that damn football in your hands and your life depends on it. Or you won't live to act on those empty threats you just made to me. They know everything. And when I had to choose between my career, my family and making a new alliance, I chose them. I gave you up so fast, it was like suckin' your dick that time and as soon as you hit my warm mouth you came so quick, hmph. It was quicker than that. Run little football player, because I hear that defenses hit hard. Oh, they are coming for your ass and I hear when they find you it might just be the last time anyone, and I do mean anyone sees you or even thinks of you." Toni laughed out loud.

"What's this? No words. Aaron are you ok, did I say something wrong? You look like you've seen a ghost." Toni said as she rubbed my arm and walked away. "Take care Aaron and thanks for everything." She continued as she waved good-bye and entered the elevator.

I could feel my blood pressure. I grew hot and a wave of sweat poured over me. Did she say they were coming for me? That could only mean that Que and Jay had been let out of prison. Suddenly, I felt dizzy; I couldn't see. I stood there trying to collect my thoughts but the only thing I could hear was Toni's warning. You better RUN!

RUN NIGGA, RUN!

Chapter Twenty-Six

"Izzo" - Jay Z

Que

Jay drove us back into the city. We did not stop. We were on a mission. I took the time to catch my nigga up on the plan. Thanks to Monica's diligence we were out. We had paid off the ADA and those involved with the case. It was proof that if you had enough money, freedom could be bought and what a joke the criminal justice system really was. This also meant that that punk ass bitch Aaron was fair game. He was priority number one. He was a threat that had to be dealt with. I should have done it back when I had the chance. But I had promised Anika I wouldn't harm him. That was one promise I should have broken. This time there would be no negotiating his life. It was mine to take.

Jay was on board as usual. I knew he wanted a piece of Aaron's ass too. He lost just as much as I did if not more. I can't help but think that maybe if Jay and I weren't locked up, Jay and Yazz's relationship might be on better grounds. I know these past months haven't been easy, but at least I had Anika to get through it. Jay barely had anyone. So I was sure as fuck that he was ready to do some damage to the man that was behind some of his pain.

We rode. As the mile markers and the destination signs drew us closer to Buffalo, all I could think about was seeing Anika and my boys; how much time had passed. I never wanted this for any of them. But I was free, and I would spend the rest of my life making up for lost time. And once Aaron was out of the way I would make right his wrongs. It was the only thing that kept me sane. Thinking about her smile, her laugh and the way she smelled. Our conjugal visits did nothing to quench my thirst for her. I needed her like oxygen, like the sun and water. She was the elements to my existence. This Aaron nigga was a negative space and a pain point since the beginning. If I could erase his presence, the elements would align again.

Jay

My Nigga Que filled me in on the plan. This bitch nigga Aaron had been a problem since the jump. We were finally going to put an end to him and all the drama he has caused. They should have known that they couldn't keep us down. We could have waited to fight it out it out in court. Our defense was solid, and we had managed to secure enough creditable witnesses that the prosecutor's case was falling apart anyway. But like my man said, why wait when we could get out now. Besides, I had unfinished business to tend too.

This mess with Yazz had served up many sleepless nights. As much as I wanted to blame it all on Aaron, I saw this shit happening way before the drama. The truth was things between me and Yazz have been unraveling since Detroit. I know she blames me for what happen to her. Shiid, I blame me. If only I could go back and do some things different, maybe if I hadn't allowed her to follow me, if I hadn't left her alone that day, there were so many variables that I needed to change, maybe then Yazz and I would be ok. There was just no way to turn the hands of time back. Yazz's innocence had been lost and disfigured the moment she fell in love with me. And no matter how I tried to protect her it just backfired. It was a love meant to destroy. I see that now. If only I had known before, I could have saved a soul. I could have protected a good girl from turning bad. Now, I'm left with trying to mend a wounded heart to a solider on a death march.

Aaron might not be the cause of my issues, but puttin' a bullet in him will ease the pain. Hell, Aaron's death will make everyone sleep a little easier. Shit, if Que has his way that bastard's body won't even return to dust. His death will serve as a reminder that The FAM is the most powerful drug cartel in the states east of the Mississippi River. And anyone coming up against us will be dealt with. Aaron's death will be the stuff of hood tales and legends. Yeah, the streets would remember our names, Que will have justice. That bitch ass Aaron better run. We were less than twenty minutes away from the city limits. And about twenty-five minutes away from our first stop. 54 Sussex had never been on the radar, but it is now. Whatever was behind that door better be prepared. Que and I were on the prowl. We were hunters, and the pride would soon be reunited. Together we would take down whomever was standing in our way. That Nigga better run. Run Aaron Run. The clock was ticking and you are running out of places to hide.

Chapter Twenty-Seven
"I Ain't No Joke"- Eric B & Rakim

Que

I had instructed Jay to pull over at the next exit. I could tell he was confused. But he didn't question me. I told him to pop the trunk. I walked around to the back of the Jaguar. Inside the trunk was exactly what I had requested.

"Jay" I called out.

Jay immediately came to the back of the car.

"Here, put this on." I said throwing a backpack in Jays direction. Inside was a pair of black sweatpants with the matching hoodie, a black skull cap, black leather gloves and a pair of black Timbs. It was the perfect outfit for war.

Jay and I quickly changed our clothes right there in the parking lot. The sun was setting. I forgot just how beautiful this time of day was. It was the perfect backdrop for the plan that lay ahead. I was certain I could outdo the wave of red that colored the horizon. Before the night was done, I would color the streets of Buffalo. The streets would bleed. Debts needed to be paid and I would be collecting in red.

I made the call and it was on. I had given specific instructions. It was time for action. Jay and I were back in the car and on our way to tangle with destiny. We drove the remainder of the way into town. Jay got off at the Grider Street Exit. We turned left. Sussex street was one of the last brick laid streets in the city. It was hard to be in stealth mode on this street. So, we parked a few streets over. Sleepy had arranged for us to park the Jaguar at one of the crew's houses. He would meet us there. We pulled into the driveway, the garage door opened and we pulled right in. Before leaving the car, I reached into the glove compartment and grab the two guns that were stored in there. I gave Jay one and took the other for myself.

We existed the car and went into the house. Sleepy, Mark and Binky greeted us. It was a family reunion of sorts. Binky and Mark were Anika's cousins. They worked for Sleepy back in Detroit. Sleepy didn't fuck with just anybody, so when he came home, he brought niggas he knew would have his back. He also left behind niggas he knew would handle business in his absence. It was good to be back amongst family. It felt damn good to be home. We dabbed each other up and got right to business.

"What the fuck is up with 54c Sussex? What do we know?" I asked.

"So far, nothing." Mark commented.

"Nothing Nigga? Jay questioned with a puzzled look on his face.

"Not like that." Sleepy intervened. "We couldn't find any information on the house. No owners, no mail, no utility bills, not a property tax note nothing. It's almost like the house doesn't exist except it does." Sleepy continued.

"So what you saying is the feds put a safe house right here in the middle of the hood and nobody figured this shit out until now." I said looking around at everyone's face for answers.

"Ain't that some shit. Them niggas put that muthafucka right up under our nose." Jay stated.

"Meanwhile, we searching every hotel, motel and Holiday Inn for this nigga and he been right here all this time. That shit is ingenious" Sleepy added.

"So now what?" Binky asked.

"We suit up. And go get that nigga." Jay commanded.

"Jay's right. It's time. I want that nigga dead now. Once the streetlights come on it's game time." I added. "Everyone knows what to do, right?" I asked.

They all shook their heads in unison.

We waited about an hour. The intel on the street said the house had been quiet all day. That didn't mean shit. Because until now we had no idea this house even existed. We don't have any history to go on. So no movement was just as good as movement. What got me confused is how no one noticed this nigga. Aaron was able to come and go as he please right under our nose. He would have been able to continue had this shit not come to an end. It was fucked up and only managed to anger me even more as I thought about it.

It was time. It was dark enough that we blended into the shadows on the street. We had arranged for a parked older car to be placed right down from the house just in case we needed a quick getaway. We were close enough to walk. So we broke off into groups and made our way to the address. This is when it paid to know your hood. The allies, short cuts and quick getaways made it easier to plan escape routes or even plan how to get somewhere with as little notice as possible. Jay and I had cut though a few back yards and made our way to Sussex. Sleepy managed to arrive at the back of the house at the same time. Mark and Binky were right behind us. Jay and I walked up on the porch. The bay window in the front of the house was closed tight but not locked. The front door had a lock that could easily be picked. Within a matter of seconds the door was open. Jay and I walked in and closed the door behind us.

There was evidence of someone living there. It almost looked like someone left in a hurry. Sleepy made his way in through the back door. Everything checked out from the back of the house. We heard a noise coming from upstairs. We slowly made our way to the stairs that sat in the middle of the house. It was just Mark and Binky. I forgot that we used to call them Spiderman. Them niggas could climb anything. It was good to see that they still used their talents. They had climbed the side of the house and entered the home from an open window on the second floor. There was no sign of Aaron. But we were positive that he had been there. He left traces behind. So we knew that nigga couldn't be far.

"So, now that we know Aaron aint here, what's the next step? Do you want us to wait here until he returns, or do you want us to post up and watch the house?" Mark asked.

"Naw. That nigga ain't coming back here. He knows his cover is blown. He's on the run with nowhere to go. Shut the city down. I want every police officer on the lookout for his car. I want every corner crew on the lookout. We've taken away the only spot he had to be safe. He'll run, but we will find him. Tonight. Put the word out that I'm home. Let the streets know the King is back and the reward is $50,000 for the person that delivers Aaron Preston to me. I want him now and make it known anyone aiding him will find themselves on the receiving end of my barrel." I declared.

The call immediately went out. Within minutes everyone knew I was back on the blocks. They also knew of the reward. News spread like wildfire. Everyone wanted in on the action. As much as I wanted to roam the jungle and hunt this muthafucka down, I had better make a stop. With the news of me being home, the last person who needed to hear this from the streets was Anika. Lord help me if she doesn't hear this from me first. We left the house just as quickly as we had entered it. I had to leave the hunt to my partners. I knew it wouldn't be long now. Aaron had nowhere to go and the clock was ticking. I would count the seconds until my gun met his fate. For now I need to get to Anika before the news did. Or I'd have a gun aimed at me and her emotions hurt way more than the bullet I was shooting.

Chapter Twenty-Eight
"Like You"- Bow Wow and Ciara

Que

Jay dropped me off at my house. It was just after 11 p.m. Jay pulled up to the gate. It was dark. Anika had security in place. My baby was smart as hell. I loved the way she moved. Her intelligence was just as sexy to me as her body. I checked in with security. I did not want them to announce my arrival. They opened the gate as I dabbed Jay up. I made the long walk up to house. I put the code in and let myself in. Anika had done some decorating and had managed to make the house a home. Her style was something out of those plush bougies magazines. And I loved that about her. It was class that you couldn't buy. The house smelled like freshly made cookies with a hint of cinnamon. I sat there in the kitchen for a moment taking in my surroundings. I had missed out on so much. I was finally sharing the same space my family had been gathering for months without me. I could hear the laughter and the cries in the silence. I was filled instantly with all kinds of emotions.

I heard footsteps coming down the back stairs. Before me stood a miniature version of me. He had rubbed his eyes and stood there looking at me.

"Whuz up?" I asked with a smile on my face.

"Who you nigga?" his bad ass asked.

"What you don't know who I am?" I asked as he walked closer to me.

His eyes were open wide. He relaxed his stance and examined me over. I stood there watching how he moved. From everything Anika told me about the twins I knew this was Rockmond. His demeanor told me he wasn't scared of anything; in fact, I wasn't sure he wasn't about to rush me. He approached at first like he was ready to protect his home, mother and brother. It was cute because he stood three apples high but had the presence of an old soul and swagger of someone my age.

"Dad!" he cried out as he ran toward me. His arms opened as I picked him up.

My son. My seed, the only thing I loved more than life itself. My son knew who I was. At two he knew me and we had not laid eyes on each other since he was born. I held him tight in my arms as we both allowed tears to roll down our face.

"Rockmond, right?" I held him like a teddy bear.

"Daddy, how did you know it was me?" he asked.

'I knew it was you from the moment I saw you. What are you doing up? Where's mommy?' I asked with a smile on my face.

"Mommy is upstairs. Sometimes she cry at night daddy. I don't like when mommy cry" Rocky confessed.

"Well, hopefully daddy can put an end to mommy crying. Now why dd you come downstairs?" I questioned.

"I wanted a cookie." Rockmond plead.

"If I give you a cookie do you promise to go to sleep and not wake up your brother or mommy?" I asked

Rockmond shook his head up and down as if to say yes. He showed me where the cookies were kept. I gave him two cookies and upstairs we both went.

I had dreamt of holding my sons in my arms. And finally, I was free and able to do so. Rockmond resembled me in every way. He was spitting image of a younger me. The way he held his head. His stares, that walk and his tone was as if I had birthed him. I walked holding my son as he directed me to his room.

I entered the room and there before me stood the other half of my heart. Draymond lay fast asleep. It was like looking into the mirror twice. My sons. My beautiful sons. Looking at them I had fallen in love all over again. It was like the first time I saw them when they were born. I would make up the last two years to them. I would make sure they knew I loved them every day that I walked this earth. I laid Rocky in his twin-size bed. Kissed him on the cheek and whispered good night. I walked back over to the bed with Draymond. He looked like an angel, but according to his mother they were demons. I found that hard to believe, but if they were anything like their father, hellions is what they were, I thought laughing to myself. I turned the lights off and closed the door behind me.

I walked further down the hallway. I took a long paused before entering my bedroom. It was dark but not dark enough that I could not make out the outline of my wife's body. My angel lay sleeping like the queen she was. I sat quietly on the chaise lounge just watching her. I loved everything about Anika. Even the way she tossed and turned in her sleep. Anika started to cry in her sleep. I walked over to rub her. It was something I had done many times whenever she seemed to be having a bad dream. It felt good to be this close to her without correctional officers, bars and cold concrete rooms. I rubbed and Anika instantly calmed down. Being next to her, in our house with my sons, made me want to give up everything for moments of peace and days full of love.

"Que!" Anika jumped and shouted.

"It's ok baby, I'm right here" I replied staring into her eyes.

"But… How… I don't understand." Anika questioned in her confused state.

I kissed her soft lips. "I'll explain everything in the morning." I whispered in her ear. For now I just want to hold my wife in my arms" I continued. I slipped out of my clothes and crawled into bed with Anika. I held her in my arms.

It wasn't before long that our kisses turned into passionate groping. Anika straddled me as we kissed. Her hands made their way to take hold of my manhood. It had already grown to full size. She directed my penis into her wet opening. She began to ride me slow and soft as we kissed. It was the welcoming home gift I had longed for. Daddy was home and I had received two of the best gifts yet. My son knew who I was, and mommy had welcomed me home as only she could. The more she rode me the more relaxed I became. All my tension seemed to wash away. Right now, the only thing that mattered was this and I needed to handle this, and she needed to handle me.

Chapter Twenty-Nine
"Heaven Sent" - Keisha Cole

Anika

I hated getting up. It felt like forever and a day since Que held me in his arms or just being able to make love to my husband without the leash that he had been tethered to. It was such a beautiful surprise. I wasn't happy that he kept the secret but I was happy that he was home and that was all that mattered. I had dreamt this day would come sooner than later. When I was unable to get to Aaron, I thought I had missed my chance to help Que. All the money in the world seemed useless if I couldn't have him by my side. He promised me last night that never again would he allow anything or anyone to separate us like that. I believed him. It was something in Que's eyes, he was vulnerable, and his words were pure. I knew he meant those words. With my hand on his heart, the oath meant everything to me. It was the only promise I would hold him to. He had never promised anything to me before. But this, he meant that shit.

I left Que sleeping like a baby. I had the nanny take the boys to the park while I ran to the grocery store. I figured this gave Que an opportunity to rest up before either the boys or the streets got a hold of him. I knew he was on a mission to deal with Aaron, but if the twins got a hold of their daddy, he was in for a fight. They would tire his ass out so fast. I wanted to hurry up so that I would not miss the happy reunion. I knew the boys would recognize their father. There wasn't a day that went by that I did not share pictures or talk about Que to them. I reminded them just how much they favored their dad, how he named them and why. They were his warriors and heirs to the kingdom. I wanted them to know that their father loved them and there wasn't a time he wasn't thinking about them. Distance and time wouldn't stop me from making sure they knew each other. Just like I gave updates to Que on his sons, Rockmond and Draymond knew how much their father cared.

I made my way around the grocery store. I wanted to grab a few things I knew Que needed, and food for a family dinner. I had planned on cooking a special dinner for Que and Jay. The two brothers were home and it was worth a celebratory dinner. Besides it would be good to see everyone at ease even if it was only for a few minutes. I picked up a few things and I was done. I was going to stop by the mall but decided to do those errands another time. I just wanted to hurry up and get back home. My husband would be waking up soon and I did not want him worrying about me or the boys.

I headed out to the parking lot. I couldn't help but feel blessed and complete. I had everything a girl could want and then some. It brought a smile to my face as I packed the truck full of groceries. I closed the truck and immediately felt the pull of strong hands lift me up and pull me down from the clouds. My mouth was covered so I could not scream. I had dropped my purse and keys as I tried to fight. The parking lot was still somewhat dark. There weren't many cars around. It was about 6:30 in the morning. Think Anika… You are wearing jeans, a red t-shirt with red sandals…He must be at least "6'2'" 250 lbs. Can you see the color of the car… Think Anika, don't close your eyes… No… What… is happening… I

… can't …focus…No… Aaron!… NO!... silently screamed as my eyes closed and everything went dark.

Chapter Thirty
Let Me Hold You" Bow Wow Ft. Omarion

Aaron

I got you Anika. I said kissing her on her forehead. I gently placed her in the back seat of the car. I quickly zipped tied her hands, covered her up with a blanket, got back in the car and drove out of the Wegman's parking lot, making sure no one saw me or Anika. I'm not sure how anyone could not see Anika. Her beauty was undeniable. Everyone who encountered her was overcome by her beauty. And at last she was mine. I drove down Elmwood. I got on the highway headed toward the airport. I had reserved a room at the Best Western off Genesse Street. I had my boy make the reservations under his name. I got a room on the first floor by the side door for quick access in and out. I finally had her. I couldn't wait for her to wake up and see me. We have so much to catch up on. There was so much I needed to say to her.

I made my way to the hotel. Thankfully there wasn't anyone sitting on the bench located on the west side of the building. I wouldn't want anyone to get the wrong idea when they saw me and Anika. After all she was my fiancé. I carried Anika into the side door. We were in room 128. I waved the plastic key badge pass in front of the door lock and the light lit up green. I was able to get Anika into the room safe and sound. We were home for now. Anika looked like an angel. My angel. I laid her on the bed. I had so many things to do, but first I would get her out of those dirty clothes. I liked my fiancé looking comfortable and sexy. Yeah, that's what the mood needed; Anika needed to be sitting pretty when she woke up. I'm sure she gonna love the outfits I picked for her. She'll love the fact that I remember her favorite shops, clothing designers and even her bra size. I had everything planned. Soon Anika and I would be leaving Buffalo and never returning.

Anika woke up finally. "There, there sweet girl. Don't be worried. I'm here." I whispered in her ear. I had dressed her in this sexy little lace teddy. It showed just enough of her curves. Her breast filled the cups of the teddy with ease. It stretched out the lace so that you could see the flower details. She was gorgeous. I could not take the chance that she would scream, so I had taped her mouth closed. Even so she was a sight for sore eyes. And she was finally mine.

I laid next to Anika. She wiggled and squirmed, but it was only because she was uncomfortable in a strange bed. I could tell she was excited to see me. Our reunion brought tears to her eyes. I was happy that she was happy. It wouldn't be long before we were both living the life that was meant for us. Far from the cold weather of Buffalo and from that asshole Que. Anika was so sexy laying there I couldn't help myself. I just had to touch her. If felt good to be close to her. Her soft body and those smooth lips, it was just like I remembered. We were finally together. Anika was all mine. And no one was ever gonna take her away from me again.

Chapter Thirty-One
"Numb/ Encore" -Jay Z featuring Linkin Park

Que

I woke up to a completely empty house. It was not what I was expecting, but knowing Anika, she went to the grocery store and was planning some elaborate dinner. The boys must be with the nanny. There was no way Anika would have taken both boys with her this morning. I just don't know how she does it. Anika has been managing our family and household and business all by herself for almost two years. She was my hero, the love of my life I thought to myself as I walked through the house to see what else Anika had done to it.

The sunlight shining through the windows didn't do the home justice. Anika had spared no expense decorating our home and tastefully too. It wasn't too much; it was classy and unique just like her. I had made my way to the kitchen. I thought it would be a good idea for me to make breakfast for everyone. It would be a great surprise and ice breaker for the boys. I decided to make pancakes, eggs and bacon. I felt at home in the kitchen. I used to cook for Anika often. Plus, breakfast was something even I couldn't mess up.

I had finished cooking breakfast as the nanny and the boys returned home. It was the reunion I had waited for. They stood there looking at me. I heard Rockmond say "I told you I saw daddy last night" to his brother. I squatted down to their size. Before I could even get a word out my arms were full of mini me's. Draymond and Rockmond had rushed to me with arms wide open. My heart overflowed with love. It was the energy that I needed, the reaction that told me they forgave me for missing hugs and kisses over the past nineteen months. It told me that my wife had kept her promise to me. She taught them who I was and apparently, they learned me. Knew my face, my voice, my behaviors, my mannerisms because lord knows they were made in my image. It was everything. I now knew what I had to do from this point forward. My princes would be raised to be kings. They would dominate and conquer. I would give them the world and more. I would do better, be better for them. It was my responsibility. One I could not take lightly. I held them and breathed in my future, my past and present. It was the gift I was given, and I accepted it. I would love and live for them always.

Over breakfast we, we got acquainted. Draymond was reserved. Rockmond asked question after question. We laughed, talked and held two-year-old conversations. We made memories. I watched them as they moved about and talked to each other. Their bond was so natural and strong. It was like they could read each other's thoughts. Like I was the odd man out at times. They were strong and independent. The way they moved reminded me of me and Jay. Our brotherhood. We connected. I was in awe of them and them of me. It was a beautiful thing. I held ack my tears until I couldn't. My boys. My family. How I missed them. And in that moment, I saw the need to love and protect them with my life. I was so consumed by the time I was spending with Rockmond and Draymond that I lost track of time. Anika should have been home by now. All of a sudden, a chill came over me. It was the same feeling I had right before the wedding. The same vibe that covered me when Anika was being attacked all those years ago. Something was wrong.

    I kissed the boys and sent them upstairs to play. I had questioned the nanny about Anika's daily routine. I needed to know where she normally shopped. Did she know what she was wearing this morning when she left. If she knew if Anika carried her gun with her or in the vehicle. Most important I asked if Anika ever went out without checking in. According to the nanny, Anika always checked in even if she was stopping off somewhere other than where she stated she was going. If it wasn't business related, she was never without her sons, she stated. She gave detailed answers. I could tell Anika had trained her well. Anika and I had laid out things anyone working for us needed to know, how they needed to react, and what we wanted them to be able to do. We lived a complicated life, so their safety, our sons safety and ours was at stake. So, based on our quick conversation, I knew the nanny would give her life for my sons. She was always carrying, she knew the safe words, codes and knew where to go if something ever happened. She gave me the look. Her eyes said it all. She had taught the boys Japanese and Russian so that they could communicate in private if something ever went down or was happening. Yes, we had a plan and I was happy to see that the nanny was a true participant and a family member.

    I also knew that she read my face. She told me that she had the boys. She put the house on full lock down. Additional security was called to the house. The nanny also asked me to follow her. She led me to a new secret room Anika had installed while I was away. She instructed me to stand there and allow the laser to do the body scan. Within seconds the door slid open. Inside I found all kinds of artillery. She looked at me and said "Go. Bring Mrs. Thomas home" in her strong accent. I grabbed what I needed. I looked up the stairwell at the sounds of the boys playing. I couldn't fathom leaving them, but something was wrong. I knew it in my soul. Anika and my connection was that strong. She needed me. Love and protect was my vow, and I'll be damn if I let her down. I grabbed car keys. Once in the car I called Jay and Sleepy. I told them what I knew. Anika was wearing jeans, a red t-shirt, her hair was pulled back in a ponytail. She had her Louis Vuitton bucket letter purse and red sandals on. She was driving the White Maxima. License plate DSF916. Put the word out I said. "Find her!" I yelled out!

"Que., We're all over this. We'll bring her home" Jay said confidently.

I was silent. My heart ached and a wave of anger poured over me. I knew it was Aaron. My gun sat in the passenger seat like it was pointing in his direction. I was suffocating, with the windows open. My heartbeat could catch up to the speed of the car, I was doing speeds of 90-100mph.I dipped in and out of traffic. I was following the tracker on Anika's car. It was parked still. It hadn't moved since I keyed in its location.

"DAMNIT!!!' I yelled as I hit the steering wheel with my fist. The anger grew and grew. That muthafucka was dead on sight. I held the tears back. I just wanted Anika back in my arms. "DAMNIT!!" I yelled as I turned into Wegmans parking lot.

I arrived at the red dot on the map. It was just like I felt, something had happened. I could see Anika's keys on the ground up under the car. I hopped out of the truck and searched the area.

"ANIKA! ANIKA!!' I screamed out loud. There was no sign of her. The car still had groceries in it. And the driver side door was open. I screamed out loud as I paced back and forth with my hands on my head. I couldn't breathe, my heart ached, my head spun with a million thought of what that bastard was doing or going to do to her. "ANIKA!" I cried out loud. "NO! NO!, NO!" I repeated as I punched the window out in the car.

Chapter Thirty-Two

"Hip Hop is Dead" – Nas

Jay

"What the fuck," I said out loud. I hopped in the car and drove to the coordinates that Que sent me. That muthafucka had a death wish. He must want to die a horrible death. I pray it's not what I'm thinking, but we all knew Aaron was desperate. He was running out of options and places to hide. I had grabbed a few extra pieces. This was bad. This shit was worse than bad. I had to get to Que. I rode into town doing speeds that should have gotten me pulled over by some white cop. It was like the street had known. Hell, the word went out. Every street I passed had soldiers out on guard. The streets were hot with cars riding and lookin. No stone unturned. We needed to find Anika before something bad happened to her or before Que loses it. Who the fuck was I kidding? That nigga was already gone. Aaron was dead on sight. All I could say was he better not harm one hair on Anika.

I pulled into the Wegmans parking lot. Que's truck was blocking traffic. He was standing there with blood dripping from his hand. Aww shit. I thought to myself. Two cop cars were already there. I prayed they were on the take and worked for the FAM. I didn't have time to explain things nor did I have the patience. I pulled up and got out the car, luckily the cops were working for us. They were there not for Que, but they received a call this morning about a possible abduction. A young lady looked like she was attacked from behind. A witness stated that he was sitting in his car looking for his coupons when he looked up and saw a man in a blue foreign car pull up and place something over the lady's mouth and she fainted. He then put her in the back seat and drove off. Once the car was out of sight the old man walked over to the lady's car and picked up her purse and took it into the store. The police handed me the purse. It was Anika's. "Damnit"!" I yelled out. I could see out the corner of my eyes, Que was pacing back and forth. He had declined medical assistance. I thanked the police officer for the intel. They were going to review the stores video surveillance to see if they could get a plate number or a car make and model. I told them that was a good idea. I'd wait for them to hear what they saw. In the meantime, I needed to check on Que.

"Que." I called out "Que" I called out again as I grabbed his arm.

"What…" He replied.

Que it's me, I could see him come to. His face was heavy. His jaw was clinched tight and his demeanor was aggressive and rightfully so.

"Que, I'm going to wait for the information from the surveillance video." I said extending my hand to him. It was holding Anika's purse in it. Que looked at the purse and immediately broke down.

"I'mma find that nigga. I'mma a put a bullet in that muthafucka. His ass is mines. He better not hurt my baby girl. I swear I'mma kill his ass. I'mma kill him Jay." Que spoke with certainty.

"I know Que. Everyone is out looking for her now. We will find her I promise." I said trying to comfort him. But I knew there were no words to make this situation better. It was a waiting game now. We either needed a lead, spotted the car or someone seen them or noticed something. Either way none of us had the time or patience to just sit and wait. I just needed to keep Que as calm as I could. That was no easy task.

A few minutes passed. The same cops came over to the car. One started to rope off Anika's car. The other one walked over to the car. He had written down the license plate of the car. It was dark blue Mercedes Benz. He said he couldn't make out the drivers face but it was definitely a man, about '6'2"-"6'3" in height. He weighed about 250-260lbs. It was more than enough of a description for me to know it was Aaron. Que's face hardened as he overheard the news. It was nothing he had not already known or suspected. They just confirmed his suspicions.

"Thanks for the information officer," I said as I got ready to get back in the car.

"Yo and tell Yazz I said hello." The cocky police officer commented.

"What the fuck you say nigga," I replied.

"No disrespect man, I just helped Yazz out a few times recently. I just wanted to make sure you knew I was here to help," the officer replied.

"Yeah ok nigga. What's your name?" I asked.

"Reggie." He answered.

"Well Reggie, you can tell Yazz hello your damn self. Second remember who you work for. The next time you address me on some bull shit, think about me puttin a bullet in your chest and you never making it home after your shift. Now that's a fucking hello, nigga." I said as I drove away.

Que just looked at me. I knew that stare. I did go in hard, but that nigga had it coming. Reggie, who was that corny nigga and why would he press me about Yazz? I didn't have time for this shit right now. I'll deal with everything Yazz once all this shit with Anika was over. Right now we needed to find that asshole Aaron and fast. Before Que kill everyone in sight including me.

Chapter Thirty-Three

"You don't Want Drama" *Ball & MJG

Sleepy

It had been hours since Anika went missing. I had checked in with everyone. Monica was out there also checking and combing the streets. The streets were on high alert. The city was on lock down. It was just a matter of time before Aaron would surface and when that bitch nigga did, we were going to be all over it. I rode around hot, just looking for any sign of my cousin. I couldn't imagine what Que was going through. All I knew was that that nigga better pray we find him before Que does. Ain't no telling what Que was going to do to him. All I know is Anika better be ok. If he touched her, harmed her in any way, all bets were off. I might shoot his ass myself.

It was about 7 p.m. when I received a call form a girl I fucked with occasionally. Brenda worked at the Best Western off Genesse Street out by the airport. I started to ignore the call. I didn't have time to dick a bitch down. I had bidness to handle.

"Yo what up though," I answered the call.

"Hey daddy, it's Brenda."

"Yup, make it quick, what's up?" I asked.

"I heard you looking for a dark blue Benz plate number XFH610. Well that muthafucka been parked outside the hotel all day. I just checked the guest list. There's an AP registered here. The room confirmation was from a Cedric Jones, but the person signed AP. That mean anything to you?" Brenda asked poppin' her gum.

"Hell yeah, ma. Good job. I might have to come thru once I handle this bidness and lay that pipe on you." I said jokingly. "I'll take care of you for the information." I added.

"Ok daddy." She replied as the phone hung up.

It was game time!

Jay

Sleepy called Que and I with the news. I made a strong U turn and headed out toward the airport. Sleepy said he would take care of the rest. Yazz was on her way. Monica was at Que and Anika's house with the boys and the nanny. Que only want the core team on this. I saw the look on his face. It was war time and this time Aaron would not escape. ETA was five minutes. Que had loaded the guns and checked the barrels. We were locked and loaded. The sounds of DMX Get at Me Dog hyped us up as we drove closer to our battlefield.

I just prayed Anika was ok. Last thing we needed was for us to walk in on a DOA. For Que's sake and the twins, Anika needed to be ok. Aaron may have been desperate, but he wasn't crazy, at least not any more than he had demonstrated. He loved Anika or so he said. Let's just hope he still did and it wasn't an *I love you but I have to kill you* scenario.

Que

Jay pulled into the parking lot and we jumped out. Sleepy was waiting for us and about a second behind us was Yazz. We were all ready for some action. Yazz covered the right side door, Sleepy took the left side door entrance. Jay and I walked in the front door. Brenda had cleared the lobby. The hotel was on lock down. Luckily they weren't fully booked. There were only 20 rooms rented out. Most of them were out for the evening. It was perfect timing. We were gonna get in and out. Brenda had pointed to the hallway that Aaron's room was located. Jay and I walked slowly down the narrow walkway. There was a housekeeper cart out blocking half of the walkway. I gestured to her to keep quiet as I walked by her and flashed my gun. She quickly shut the door to the room she was cleaning and stayed inside. We made our way to the room.

Jay had grabbed the housekeeping master keys off the cart that was in the hallway. Jay slowly waved the plastic key over the door security card. The green light came on and on the count of three Jay opened the door, guns drawn.

Aaron did not notice that we had entered the room. He was on top of Anika getting ready to rape her. She was tied up. We had entered the room just in time. Watching him about to … all I could do was fire a shot. It startled him as he rolled off of Anika and onto the side of the bed. The bullet had just pierced his side. I did not want to take a chance that I'd shot Anika. I ran over to Aaron and began pistol whippin' his ass. My right hand was already busted up from punching the window out on my truck. My adrenalin was in full effect. I couldn't stop. I wanted that nigga dead.

Jay pulled me off him. He broke my trace. I had more pain to inflect on this bitch nigga. He needed to feel everything that I felt and more. He had to pay.

'Not here Que, not here!" Jay commanded.

I knew he was right.

Yazz had managed to untie Anika and cover her up with the blanket. Her eyes were filled with tears. It was the one thing I hated most. Seeing Anika cry. I felt my fist ball up all over again. I looked at Aaron and jammed my gun down his throat. He gagged as I cocked the trigger. With every breath my face tightened, my heart skipped beats and all I wanted was to end this shit. I could feel my veins popping from the adrenalin or from my anger.

"Que! Jay cried out, "Let's go!"

I hit that nigga one last time as Sleepy grabbed him and wrapped him up in the sheets. I put Anika in my arms and carried her out of the room down the hallway and outside to the car. She held on to me tight. I wiped her tears away and assured her that it was over. I whispered over and over that I had her, and that no one would ever hurt her again. I promised. I placed her in the back seat and sat with her. I held her tight. I would never let her go again.

Jay and Sleepy loaded Aaron into Sleepy's trunk. Just as fast as we entered the hotel, we were out. Yazz followed close behind us. She took care of the video tape and the housekeeper. She handed Brenda a stack of money for her assistance and silence. There was no need to spill innocent blood. All parties understood what would happen if anyone spoke a word of what they saw here today. It didn't matter that the housekeeper didn't speak fluent English. She understood the weapon Yazz showed and the money she took. It was easy math.

We drove back into the city limits. There was a warehouse downtown near the waterfront that we used for such occasions. I knew that was where

Jay was headed. I wanted to drop Anika off, but she insisted on coming. I was ready to end this shit once and for all.

Sleepy

I got that muthafucka out the trunk of the car. This bitch ass nigga just pissed himself. I can't stand a wannabe gangsta. This nigga gone plead for his life, yet he was about that life when he was protected by the Feds or when Que's ass was locked up. Now that we pulled his card, this nigga bitched up like a little hoe. I just shook my head as I punched him in the mouth. "Shut the fuck up nigga." I laughed out loud.

You gonna take this ass whoppin' and die. I continued. I dragged him into the warehouse. His blood left a trail of DNA evidence behind us. I strung him up on the chains and pulley that ran down from the ceiling.

"You just wait right here. Que and Jay will take it from here" I warned as I punched him in the ribs. I was certain I had cracked something. You could hear the pain with every breathe Aaron inhaled.

Jay

I knew I wouldn't be able to stop Que. Hell, I'm not sure I wanted to. This nigga had it coming to him. First, he has Que and I arrested and charged. He was gonna do his damnist to see to it that Que and I do time for a murder we didn't commit. Then, he kidnapped Anika and was planning to god know what next.

I poured gasoline over Aaron's hanging tattered body. I wasn't sure what Que was planning, But I was going to be prepared. I had to shock that nigga to get him up. His body wiggled like an animal that was getting ready to be skinned alive.

"So, you're up now" I questioned.

"No words… How disappointing this encounter is. I was hoping that you would at least put up a fight You're just a typical bitch nigga. You tried it," I said as I shocked him again and piss rolled down his legs.

Aaron hung there like the pathetic piece of shit he was. It was sad. He was willing to give up his career, and his life for someone that didn't belong to him. All it caused was drama and pain. And when it was all said and done, he was not walking out of here. I'm not even sure he would ever be seen or heard from again.

All this kept reminding me of was when them fools took Yazz. I worried, cried and prayed for her safe return. I got her back, but it was never the same. I hoped this interchange did not damage Anika the way it had done Yazz. I'm happy we found her, and once Que puts a bullet in this nigga, we can finally put the past behind us.

Que

I knew Jay and Sleepy would handle business for now. My primary concern was Anika. I had to make sure my baby was ok. The more I played back the events of the day the sicker I felt and the angrier I became. I needed to know. I just couldn't bear to ask. But seeing Anika laying there tied up and helpless with Aaron straddling her. It took me back to what happen to Yazz and even worse that punk muthafucka Bam. I had all these feeling of anger and wrath washed over me. Anika lay on the cot and all I could do to keep my sanity was punch the wall. It was the only way to release the fire that burned within.

FUCK!!! I screamed aloud. I paced back and forth only stumbling over my last thoughts that prevented me from creating a steady pace. There were no words I could whisper, no song to sing or sentiment I could express to Anika to take away her pain. But I was going to do my best. That muthafucka was going to pay. I pulled my gun out from under my shirt. The steam that fueled the flames inside of me exited my body as I exhaled and collected my thoughts. I had one agenda; kill Aaron. I walked out of the room without looking at Anika. My stride was cool and focused. I had two loaded guns and I intended to use every clip I had on me. But first I would torcher him the way I assumed he had done to Anika.

I could smell the stench of gasoline the closer I came to Aaron's hanging matted body. I wasn't sure Aaron deserved death by fire. It seemed too easy, too quick for the man that has made my life a living nightmare. I wasn't sure there was a death imagined yet that fit the crimes he had committed. But whatever I decide, with his last breath he would wish he never met Anika or broke a promise to me. This nigga would die by my hands and serve as a constant reminder to everyone that I am not to be fucked with. As I moved closer to administer the pain he caused me, my stride was interrupted.

"Que," I heard Anika whisper as she mustered up enough energy to make her way into the room.

"Anika go lay back down," I commanded.

"Que, no." Anika spoke clearly. Ignoring me as she moved closer.

"ANIKA!" I yelled causing her to stop in her place.

Jay and Sleepy stood there in silence. Aaron had lifted his head up just enough to see Anika's face. His arrogance allowed him to crack a half smile, that caused me to slap the shit out of him.

Chapter Thirty-Four
"You can't play with my YoYo" – YoYo

Anika

"QUE!" I forcefully yelled back at him forcing him to turn around and look at me.

I stood there in a bra and panty set that Aaron had dressed me in. I was past ashamed. I was beyond upset; I was scorned. I had once loved this man. I had once saw me having a life with him. I loved him, but I was not in love with him. I gave him space in my heart. I had prayed for forgiveness and asked that he find the power to heal. I wanted him to find happiness and acceptance of who he was. But instead this nigga decided to return. He decided to harm me, take away the one man who truly loved me. He would have my sons become statistics as their father sat rotting inside a prison cell. He would see me struggle to manage as a single parent and wish for my dismay.

The anger grew inside of me with every step I took. Yazz had tried to pull at me. I saw her out the corner of my eye. I knew she had good intentions, but good intentions never worked when you're a part of the streets. I now know that. Look at what happen to Ayanna. She had good intentions. She loved a man that wasn't hers. She let him go only to find someone that loved her the way she deserved and for what. She was now my guardian angel. I lost my sister because of good intentions. Look at Monica, she let her guard down and allowed love in and what good did it do her. She had good intentions, but where was the love in the way Mario died. Good intentions didn't stop what happen to Yazz. It didn't save her from all the pain and tears she shed. Now look at her, she's a hollow shell of the women she used to be. So, what did we owe to good intentions, … not a godamn thing.

Yazz had reached for me again. "Get the fuck off of me Yazz" I said firmly.

I saw her back away. Sleepy started to approach me. I held up my gun and he knew I meant business. Not that I would shot him, but when I said step the fuck back, he knew enough to know that I wasn't playing. Jay stood off to the right of Que with is hands up as if to say I give up. The air was stiff and silenced played like light dinner music.

There I was standing face to face with the two men I had given myself to. One I loved and one I was madly in love with. One who wanted to be my savior and the other played savior. I wasn't torn between the two, I had chosen my king. Yet I needed to make it know. My destiny was already set. I was ready to fully defend my family and The FAM. Aaron was an obstacle that needed to be dealt with. He posed a threat to me, Que, my sons and business. When Auntie Rose slapped me into reality, and I assumed my rightful seat at the family table, I knew this day would come. I could not fight what had to happen. Nor did I want to. I wasn't the weak girl Que had to save before. I wasn't the helpless women, he married. I had grown in the last two years, forcefully, but willingly.

I had accepted the consequences of my actions when I took my seat as the head of The FAM. There was no turning back now.

Without hesitation, I pulled the trigger. My aim was intentional and deliberate. I pulled it again. And again, and again. I watched as Aaron's body absorbed the blow of each bullet. There were no words, just the echoes of the bullets piercing through his skin. His eyes glared deep into my soul. He was once the man I thought of and he morphed into a demon haunting my dreams. And again, I pulled the trigger. His smile quickly mimicked the pain I felt over the past months. His blood poured out in sacrificial rain. I had forgiven him for everything he had done to me. I prayed that he finally find peace. And I hoped that someone would cry tears of love for his soul. All I knew was that it would no longer be me. I pulled the trigger emptying the clip. I gave him the final piece of me. My innocence will be buried with Aaron's soul.

I looked around at the crowd of familiar faces. I was done playing the damsel in destress. I had worn many hats and that one had become my least favorite. I had earned every stripe of respect. I had lead The FAM into a new era. There was no room for softness. There was no need for approval. I was and I am the women I wanted, needed and had to be. Que walked over to me and kissed me hard and long. My body caved into his arms as he picked me up and carried me away.

Chapter Thirty-Five
"Dangerously in Love 2"- Beyoncé

Jay

It had been a few days since the event with Anika. And just as many days since my release from the jail cell. I thought being home would have made me happy, instead I felt like I was walking on eggshells. The home I once shared with Yazz had somehow become cold and empty even though we were both occupying the same space. There were pockets of silence even though I was sure I was crying out loud. I didn't even know where to begin. The last conversation with Yazz was right before I was released. We agreed to put things on hold until all of this was behind us. Now that the storm had passed, neither one of us wanted to comb through the remains. It seemed we both were scared that the damage was irreconcilable.

I found myself sitting in the dark wishing Yazz would be my light again. Staring into space, I wished I could reach out to her and hold her. Kiss her lips the way I had stolen that kiss during our last encounter. I need her. But I know I had let her down. I knew that this life I lead would eventually eat away at her. I just never dreamed that it would have changed her the way it had. It broke my heart every time I looked into her beautiful eyes and saw the darkness that was once so innocent and full of hope. I fucked up and I would never forgive myself.

Yazz

All I keep thinking about was our last encounter. He walked away. It felt like he turned his back on me when I needed him most. Right when I was ready to open up. There was so much I needed to say, but it fell on deaf ears. He couldn't see me and I can't hear him. It seemed like we were on two different paths headed in the same direction, lost looking for each other but unable to connect. I watch him now and I just don't know if I can ever get back to the woman he loves. I'm not sure she even exists anymore. Maybe I shouldn't feel bad for evolving, maybe this is who I'm supposed to be. Maybe this is who I was all along and just didn't realize it until now.

The past few nights we slept in separate rooms. Not because I wanted to, but I'm afraid what would happen if we found ourselves in a vulnerable state. Nothing said rejection like being naked and afraid without the comfort of his arms. The truth is I loved him, but there was so much baggage. So much had happened. I blamed him, myself, my heart and anything else that seemed to lead me down this path. I wanted to stop placing that on him, but I couldn't. I loved a man that could not protect me the way I needed him to. I loved a man, that I knew would eventually hurt me. The way he sat there looking at the bitch that day I showed up at the prison to visit. I saw it. It was the same look he used to give me. That spark of light I used to be for him, she had dimmed. He can say it was nothing, but I felt it. I saw it. It was the last shock to my heart. I had taken and endured enough for this love and all it had done was let me down. I wanted Jay, but maybe enough was enough. Maybe it was time we say ….

Jay

"Yazz, excuse me can we talk?" I asked knocking on the bedroom door.

I could tell that she was in deep thought.

"Sure," Yazz replied.

I walked over to the side of bed she was sitting on. "I just wanted to clear the air. We said we would talk after things settled, well it's been a couple days." I started to say before I started to choke up. "Listen Yazz, I love you. I always have and always will." I paused. "I just need to know that you can forgive me. Forgive me for not protecting you. For dragging you into this world. For all the fucked-up shit that has happened. I just can't take knowing that I'm the cause for all your pain and sadness."

"Jay, it's you, it's me. I have no idea who I am right now. So much has happened, I've been blaming everyone but me. No one told me to follow you. I could have easily stayed here when you left. I chose to go. I chose this lifestyle. I thought that's what I needed to do to be with you. Thought that if I didn't you would leave me. That you wouldn't love me." She said as the tears began to surface.

"Yazz I could never ask that of you, I loved you before all this. I would have continued to love you. I never wanted this life for you, hell, I didn't want it for me once I met you. You made me see a future outside of this world. Don't you see that?" I spoke reaching out for her hand. Just that simple touch warmed my heart.

"Jay" Yazz spoke softly.

"Yes" I answered.

"That girl, the one I saw that day…" she continued

"She means nothing to me. It's only been you. You are all I need. You are all I want." I confirmed as I looked into her eyes. I was searching for that hope that used to get me through some many nights.

"Jay, I'm not stupid. I saw the way you looked at her." Yazz rebutted

"She meant nothing" I said as I gently grabbed Yazz's chin and drew her closer to me. "Nothing" I repeated. As I kissed her.

Yazz

It was like he had washed away the darkness with just that one kiss. I wanted to believe him. I needed to believe him. Jay had never lied to me and I doubt that he would start now. He kissed me over and over. With each kissed I felt the cleansing of regret. The washing away of the guilt. I wanted him. I needed him. I loved him and I knew that from day one. I closed my eyes and let go of the pain. Jay looked at me for approval. I needed him to quench my thirst. It had been so long since we made love. So long since he touched me without rushing, without worry, without hesitation. My body ached for him. My insides throbbed as he undressed me. I found my body arching and twisting in positions as he reacquainted himself with me. Jay kissed every part of me. His lips just as soft as I remembered. His body was so warm. The way he held me in his arms told me he would do his best to protect me. I believed him.

His tongue played me like a sweet slow song. I matched him stroke for stroke as our bodies collided. He held my hair in his hands. He twisted it to revel my neck as he sucked and kissed me. I rode and bucked to remind him of the women he had in his corner. I was his ride or die. I would never leave his side. We moved as one. There in the darkness, our light shined. It was pure and honest, and it was us. I loved him and he loved me. I would hold on to this moment. The way I pierced my nails into his back. We sexed each other until the doubt and fears were released. Until we both knew where we stood in each other's hearts. It was a beautiful imperfect bound.

He saw me now for who I was, and I heard his cries. It was a beautiful imperfect song.

"Just keep loving me" I whispered.

"Don't give up on us Yazz, I need you baby" he replied.

"I love you "I uttered

"I love you" Jay said looking me in the eyes.

I believed him.

And I know he believed me too.

Chapter Thirty-Six
"Bonnie and Clyde" Jay Z

Que

It had been a few days since Anika's ordeal. It seemed like she was ok. She didn't want to talk about it. So, I left that shit right where we left it. I wasn't sure how I should feel about what went down. On the inside I clapped. What Anika did was on some gangsta shit. My baby just killed the nigga that had been the source of all the drama we had been through. She shot the fuck out of that bitch ass muthafucka. On the other hand, that was Anika's first kill. The first is always the hardest. Taking a life is not something I nor anyone should take lightly. I'm not out here trying to play god. I know just how precious life is. Especially now that I have three to be accountable for. The streets don't care, if your number gets called, or you get caught up in some dumb shit, then that's your ass. Aaron got what he had coming to him. I just didn't think Anika should have been the one to do it.

Anika was all smiles. She did the wifey thing with ease. The way she cared for my sons gave me a whole new outlook on motherhood. But occasionally, I would catch a glimpse of sorrow in her eyes. This was the very thing I had wanted to protect her from. I was the one in the relationship that we supposed to have dirty hands. I had blood on me since I was a youngin. No killing didn't come any easier, but I had to do what was needed to protect the cause. Now the urgency was beyond the drug game. I had a family to protect. I would pull that trigga without hesitation. No questions asked. I couldn't wash away the things I had done. There was no soap or bleach strong enough to take the spots and blemishes away. But Anika was spotless, unblemished, until now. I didn't want my necessary to become her every day.

I would let it go for now. I wouldn't be her husband if I wasn't concerned. But damn my baby did that shit. She did it like a G. I wasn't sure if she was trying to prove something to someone else or herself. But she had already had my respect. Now I know she earned the respect of everyone else with just that one act. She's the head of one of the most powerful drug families in the states. Now everyone knew who she was and what she was capable of. She was a force all her own. And the best part, she was all mines. She was my ride and I would die for her. The perfect union.

Anika

I woke up and made breakfast for my family today. I just loved watching Que interact with his sons. I had waited so long for this day. The way he looked at them, spoke to them, and the way they just gelled, warmed my heart. The boys took to their father and had finally found their lost best friend. It was bond that was always there without me knowing. As for me, I was just enjoying the view. I had become the odd person out. But I did not mind. I loved being the queen amongst the men. It was my job to take care of them, you know do the motherly stuff even when it came to Que. He was the biggest kid of them all. This was the softer side of him that the streets were not privileged to see.

Que kept asking me if I wanted to talk. Talk about what? I had nothing that I needed to talk about. What he really wanted to know was how was I doing since I shot Aaron. The truth was I was fine. At first, I could not believe that I had killed someone. It went against everything that my mother had instilled in me. It was a sin according to the holy bible and yet Aaron put me in a predicament that left me no choice. It was a sin to do it and a sin not to. At least that's how I saw it. Whatever reservations I had before I pulled the trigger, all went away once I saw Aaron's defeated body hanging there in the warehouse. I was sincerely ok. I just wanted everyone else to be ok with what I had done.

The more I thought about what had happened, the more it felt like destiny. Here I was the head of a notorious crime family and I had yet to have my first kill. I had only pulled the trigger at the shooting range. I had plenty of practice aiming and shooting the paper target. If I wasn't going to ever shot the gun then what was all the practicing for? There was no way I was going to be the head of something this big and expect not to get mt hands dirty at some point. I also knew there was only so many times that I could wait on being rescued. At some point I was going to have to woman up and take charge and control my destiny. Which was what I had done with Aaron. Enough is enough. I just needed everyone else to be ok with what went down. Besides, I was evolving and becoming stronger. There was nothing wrong with that, especially now that I was a wife and mother. I was strong not because I wanted to be but because I had to be. My family and our way of life depended on it.

Chapter Thirty-Seven

"Crying out for me" – Mario

Sleepy

It had been a couple of weeks since all that shit went down with ole' boy. Que insisted that Anika was ok. I had stopped by to see my lil' cousins and visit my Anika. She seemed alright, but I knew she wasn't, hell nobody is after taking their first life. That shit sort of hunts you for a while. Your first body is always the most difficult. But Anika was putting up a great front. She had the house smelling all good and shit. She was smiling and all jokes, but deep down I really did hope she was ok.

Monica on the other hand, wasn't at all acting like herself. There wasn't any fast talk, sexual innuendos or advances. Normally this was how Monica engaged a nigga daily. It was something I became accustomed to and even looked forward to. When Mo would cut up, it made for a much more exciting day. Even the way she looked most days. It was a calmer her. No ass showing shorts, no heels or low-cut shirts. She was wearing sweats and tank tops with sneakers. Fortunately for me, Mo looked sexy in whatever she wore, but it was just different. I could tell something was going on with her. She may not want to talk to me about it, but with everyone dealing with shit, Jay and Yazz and Que and Anika, I may be the next best person to lay that burden on. After all, we were partners. I was going to make it my business. Shit, I did care.

Mo and I were driving around, making our normal stops. She sat there quiet. The radio was playing all kinds of jams that should have had her dancing in her seat, but she had no reaction. It was getting late, and I was getting hungry.

"Yo Mo, I'm about to order something. You want anything?" I asked.

She shrugged her shoulders and gestured no. I just shook my head as I got out of the car making our last stop. I had returned to the car just in time to catch a tear streaming down Monica's face. I pretended not to see it as she turned her head so that would not notice. We rode in silence as I stopped at Kim's Kitchen right there on E. Ferry and Fillmore. There were a few dudes I knew in there. I dabbed them up said a few words, grabbed my order and was out.

I drove back to my place. Now, I wasn't living like Que and Jay. I preferred to be where the action was. It kept me closer to the streets and my ear to the ground. We pulled into my house on Moselle. It was an old family house. When I decided to come back to help Anika out, this was the first place I wanted to be. I had so many memories of growing up here. All the parties, the neighborhood cookouts, shooting ce-lo at the corner, messing with the hotties that strolled by. Hell, those were the good ole days before I even caught a case, let alone a body. This was one of the few places I felt safe.

With all the chaos that happen now on the block, this was home. Plus, no one was stupid enough to fuck with this address. They knew and if they didn't, they knew someone that did. Like I said, I felt safe. I pulled up, got out and walked around to the passenger side door. I opened it for Mo. She was in deep thought. I had interrupted it.

"Where are we?" she asked as she observed her surroundings. She looked a little concerned, but she acted hard.

"We at my place." I responded.

"I thought you were like Jay and Que living out in the boonies and shit" Mo replied.

"So what you tryna say. You think a nigga gotta spend all his chips? I ain't no bougie ass nigga," I said laughing.

"I know that, but I at least thought you lived in a nicer neighborhood." She said laughing back at me.

"Yo I can drop your ass right back at your crib! Shid you ain't gonna have a nigga feeling some kinda way!" I said as I walked away.

"Naw, we good." Monica said laughing as she followed me up the front porch and into the front door.

I must admit, Monica was the first girl I had over here since I came back. Normally if I was fuckin' a girl or for my random booty calls I would either go back to their place or to the telly. I was not ever gonna let them hoes know where I lay my head at. Next thing you know, they be bringing that drama to my doorstep. I ain't got time for that shit. I lead Monica into the Livingroom as I turned on the lights. It was the typical

Bachelors pad. I had a matching black leather coach, love seat and recliner anchored by a patterned area rug. There was a large TV that was connected to my PlayStation and Xbox. Mo quickly made herself at home. She had kicked off her sneakers and relaxed on the coach. I made my way to the kitchen and prepared two plates of Chinese food. I knew enough to order plenty of food for the both of us. Monica had a way of saying she wasn't hungry and then asking for whatever I had. Normally it would piss me off. I learned to just be prepared. And if she truly wasn't hungry what's a few dollars. I could either eat it later or throw that shit away.

I came back into the room carrying the two plates. I bypassed the living room and went straight to the dining room. I lit an incense. I noticed that Mo had that same look on her face that I caught a glimpse of earlier.

"Yo Mo, come grab a bite to eat! "I called out to her. It snapped her back into the present. She got up and followed my voice. Mo sat down at the table. I had went back to the kitchen and grabbed two glasses.

'What are you drinking?" I asked.

"It don't matter. Whatever you have" she answered.

I made my way back to the table. With two glasses of water.

"Nigga, what you ask me what I want to drink if this all you got?" she said taking a sip.

"I got liquor. I don't have any juice or Kool-Aid. I'm not eating Chinese food and drinking liquor. You tryna have my ass sitting on the toilet all night. No sir" I clowned her.

My smart remark made her crack a smile. I sat down at the table. We ate in silence. But I could not ignore the absence of our normal banter any longer

"Mo, what up lady?" I inquired.

"Nothing" she replied.

"I can see that. But for real, what's bothering you?" I asked in a playful manner.

"Nigga, I'm not about to have a Rickie Lake moment with you" she clowned.

"Why not? We cool. I thought we could talk about anything. You my girl, right?" I asked.

"Sleepy, we good. I just got a lot on mind. Not much to talk about." Monica insisted

"Lies!" I rebutted

"What the fuck you talking about? I'm not lying about shit." Monica retaliated as she looked away from me and took another bite of her food.

"You been walking around here lookin all sad and shit for days now. A nigga just concerned. You not acting like the Monica I've come to know and love. That's all." I confessed.

Monica broke away from the table. She turned her back to me.

"Yo Mo, did I say something wrong?" I asked as I moved after her.

I walked up behind her. I gently turned her around to see the tears that had flooded her face.

"Yo Mo, whatever it is we can fix it. You know I got your back" I whispered to her.

I went to wipe her face and she pulled back.

"What the fuck Monica! I'm trying to look out for you" I said annoyed but concerned.

I walked closer to her. This time I could sense that she was not going to run and hide.

I wrapped my arms around her. She just cried. There was silence. I picked her up in my arms and carried her to the couch. We sat on the coach with me holding her and Mo trapped in my arms. The smell of Egyptian Musk filled the house. Our food had gotten cold. It didn't matter. What mattered was finding out how I could help Mo. If it meant that I hold her and make sure she's ok, then that's what a nigga gone do.

About a half hour past. The tears were starting to dry up and I could tell by Mo's breathing that she was gaining control of her emotions. I waited until I thought she would be open to talking. Before I could even say a word, Mo spoke.

"What is wrong with Me Sleepy?" she questioned.

"What do you mean? I countered.

"I had a good man, but he just gave up. Mario just gave in, he didn't even fight for me." Monica started to open up. "He left me. Now, I'm alone. Every guy I meet, ain't worth the time, wouldn't understand me or just out for sex. Why am I not worth loving?" Monica cried.

"Oh, Mo. I don't think that it's that simple. What I do know is that Mario loved you. He used to tell me about you every chance he got. You made that thug see a future past the street game. That's how I knew you were special." I stated as I wiped the remainder of her tears away.

"Now, I don't know why Mario did what he did, what I'm sure of is that he loved you. But Mo, if I was in Mario's shoes, I could never leave you. I would never want to do anything to hurt you. You are an amazing strong independent woman. You know who you are and what you want. Any real man would be honored to have you by their side." I confessed.

Monica looked up at me. I wasn't sure if she believed me, but it was the truth. I had grown to know and love Monica. It was easy to see what Mario saw in her. She truly was amazing.

"Then why am I still alone? Why?" she asked.

"Maybe the right man hasn't come along. Maybe…" I paused.

I sat there holding her. I was staring at my equal. It pained me to know that she did not know her worth. She was beautiful. I didn't know who had broken her heart and left her feeling like she was unworthy, but I wanted to tell him he was wrong. Monica was every bit worthy. From her eyes to her smile. She was intelligent and hood. It was the perfect storm, but one that could be calmed. Her classy, sassy ways made me smile. She was special. I needed her to know that.

Without warning I kissed her. I shouldn't have but I did. It was something I had wanted to do from the very beginning. Her lips were soft and full. She kissed me back. I was breaking all the rules and this time I did not even regret it. Monica sat straddling me on the couch as our tongues danced in each other's mouths. She tasted so sweet. It was venomous poison with no cure. I had been warned and yet I wanted the forbidden fruit.

I just wanted her to be ok. I just wanted her to know that I see her. The real her and she was perfect. I wanted to tell her that the right person would find her and when he did, he would accept her too. I wanted her to be open to love one day and not play herself so short. She was worth it. I kissed her and hoped that he heard my thoughts.

Before I could even think, I had picked her up and taken her to my bed. Our lips locked. I held her in my arms. We parted lips. Monica undressed. Her silhouette was designed in the perfect letter S. I ran my fingers along her curves. It was a road map I wanted to learn. I had taken off my t-shirt and unzipped my jeans. I stood there watching over Monica. The way she moved, the way the streetlight echoed through the blinds and danced on her skin made me sing Hallelujah. It was the first for me and the first for her. Monica lay naked in my arms. First, I had never had a woman in my bed. Second, I would never lay naked next to any bitch and not fuck. But Monica wasn't just any bitch. She was my partner, my girl and most importantly my friend. I loved her. Hell, I think all the resisting I did made me fall in love with her.

Monica rested in my arms. I kissed her neck and back. She would roll over and face me. We locked lips over and over until she rested her head on my chest and drifted off to sleep. We lay there wanting more, but just allowed the moment to happen. Monica's heart had been broken one time too many. Even the strongest woman will crack under pressure. She needed to mend. I wanted to be the glue that could make her whole again. What we found out was we had been more than friends for a while now. But what she needed was actions. No more words. She needed to feel the love of a man and know his actions matched. Tonight, I would start to prove to her she was worthy. We both fell asleep holding on to each other. It was the best night sleep I had had in a long time.

Chapter Thirty-Eight
"Pass the Courvoisier" – Busta Rhymes

Monica

It was well overdue. Que and Jay had been out of them jumpsuits for a month and we had yet to celebrate. So tonight was gonna be on and poppin'. Anika had planned a family dinner at Buffalo's Chop House. They had reserved the entire dining room for the night. Anika had request that all the Generals and Capos be in attendance for dinner. So, niggas from all over the country were coming into town. She had reserved 4 floors at the Walden Millennium Hotel by the Galleria Mall. She had planned an elaborate party at the Marriott Downtown by the waterfront. Everyone was supposed to be in the house for that. It was going to be the shit.

I had shit to do before tonight. Sleepy said he had the routes today so I could go get ready. I had a hair appointment right after I finished with my nails and feet. Lisa was almost done adding the latest fades to my nails. I loved the bling and all the other stuff she did in her designs. She had a bitch waving her hands all the time, I thought to myself as I laughed. "Perfect" I said as she finished. I hoped the nail color matched the dresses Anika had custom made for us. Anika asked that Yazz and I meet her at her house around five to get ready. She had a surprise for us for tonight. Mind you it was an All-white party. Knowing Anika, I guess we were going to be standout at the event and why not, we were her right-hand bitches. If she order custom dresses for us, this only meant that hoes was wearing something grand.

I would head over to Anika's after I was done getting my hair done. Had to admit, I was lookin forward to tonight. It had been a while since we all were able to let loose and have some fun. It was going to be good to see everyone enjoying themselves. Especially Anika and Que. Lawd knows they been through enough this year. Hell, what am I saying, we all have been through enough. It was about time things get back to normal, or as normal as things could for us.

Yazz

I woke up in Jay's arms. It was like old times. I cooked him breakfast. We ate breakfast in bed, cuddled some more and then we each had to head out. Jay and Que's homecoming party was tonight. It was the talk of the streets. It was the hottest ticket in town and if you weren't on the invite list then your ass was out of luck. Anika wanted a drama free evening. She was kicking it off with dinner and then the party. She had asked Jay and Que what they wanted to eat and both said they wanted a good steak, so Anika booked the Chop House. She spared no expense. She booked the entire 250 seats for tonight. That meant everyone in the organization that was somebody would be in attendance. No excuses.

I was excited about tonight. It had been so long since we partied. Now that Anika was married with kids, the only time I saw her was when I went out to the house or we had business to handle. Monica was so busy with Sleepy that I never really had a moment alone with her anymore. And I don't know what was going on with the two of them, but they seem a little too cozy to just be friends. Monica seemed at peace, more relaxed and not as wild as she was before. I don't know what Sleepy was doing, but his influence on her was staring to show. Hell, someone could say the same about me. I was in therapy now. I was trying to deal with the rape shituation. I needed to get that out and off me. It was all my idea and Jay supported me. It was going to be a slow process, but it was worth it. And in the process, it was helping my relationship with Jay. Things were looking up.

As I headed out to Anika's, I couldn't help but think about where we all started. We were the magnificent foursome. The only one missing was Ayanna. I missed my sister so much. Sometimes I could still hear her voice. She helped keep me in line. She was my checks and balance keeper. I was grounded with her and maybe that was part of the chaos in my life. I never had the opportunity to grieve for my sister. I hadn't allowed myself to really think about what that loss meant to me. I hated that I wasn't here when that shit went down. I hated that I wasn't there to protect her. I guess it was the same feeling that Jay had for me or even Que for Anika, even how Monica was with Mario and the way Sleepy looked out for us all. We were each other's keepers. It just was how it was. We were a family, a unit all connected by the streets. For good or bad we had each other's backs. Tonight, may not be quite like old times but it would be pretty damn close. I knew Mario and Ayanna would be partyin up in heaven or down in hell with us. Either way they would be watching over us. And that way we were still each other's keepers.

Anika

I had given the twins their baths after feeding them. I read them a story as I did every night. Tonight, it came a little early. I had planned the biggest celebration I could to welcome my husband and Jay home. I had to. I had waited so long to have him home. My family was complete. Tonight was going to be just like old times. Well, maybe not quite. We each had grown so much over the past few years. We weren't the hot young tender ronies we used to be. We were still the shit, but not like before. Yeah, maybe our looks hadn't faded, but mentally and emotionally we each had been scared.

Lord knows that we each had our fair share of drama. We each made choices that led to some serious consequences. But no one said all was fair in love and these streets. We chose the paths we did, and it was up to us to make the best of our situation. If you had said to me years ago, I would be married to Que and have kids, I would have laughed in your face. I also knew what Que was about. I never wanted to live this life, but I chose love and now look at me. I'm living the life but at a cost. The same cost that Yazz paid, Monica cried over and Ayanna died for. So, tonight was about freedom. We all were finally free to be who we were. No pretenses, no judgements, just free. Just me thinking that showed maturity on my part.

I knew the girls would be arriving soon. I had custom designer dresses made for them. It was an All-white party, but what did we look like strolling up in there wearing white. We always went against the grain. Tonight, was no exception. Monica and Yazz were wearing black dresses and I of course would be wearing red. After all I was the queen. I wanted everyone in attendance to take note and see us. We were the three most powerful women in the room and on the streets. We were a force to be reckoned with on our own, but we were a hurricane together. Them niggas didn't stand a chance. We were the baddest bitches and tonight we would show up as such.

Yazz and Monica looked amazing in their dresses. Hell, we all looked sexy as hell. Monica was wearing a strapless lace body hugging dress., while Yazz was wearing a silk halter dress that had a double slit up the sides of her legs that made Athena herself nod in approval. I was wearing a red corseted strapless dress. It was a mini dress with a long ass train. It was covered in diamond accents. The dress hugged my body like a glove and when dinner was over, I would be able to remove the train. It was a showstopper. This reminded me of the many nights we would all meet up over each other's houses to get ready to go out on the town. Oh, how I missed those days. These women were my dearest and closest friends. We shared secrets and kept each other's dreams safe. Tonight, was just as much about us as it was the men in our lives. I wanted more nights like tonight. I needed more time with my sisters.

We finally made our way downstairs to the men folk. They cleaned up nicely. They each were wearing a white tuxedo. Jay and Sleepy had the black-tie ensemble that matched Yazz and Monica's dresses. Que was wear a white tuxedo jacket and shirt with a pair of red tuxedo pants with some white Italian leather shoes that were encrusted with diamonds. He was so flashy and extra. I think I'm starting to rub off on him. We looked nothing short of a million bucks. Que wanted to say a few words before we headed out. Everyone grabbed a cognac glass. We raised it to the air as Que spoke.

It was priceless. I would capture that image in my mind forever. We each took the double shot to the head and made our way to dinner. It was nights like this, that I wished never ended.

Chapter Thirty-Nine
"Lean Back"- The Terror Squad

Sleepy

Dinner was awesome. That steak was like butter but even better than that was that I had one of the baddest chic's in the game on my arm. Naw, it wasn't what you were thinking. Me and Mo were taking things slow. She wasn't in a rush and neither was I to put labels on each other. But we did have some rules. That fucking everybody shit needed to slow down. If we were going to try this relationship shit, it had to be only me and her. She agreed. I had asked Monica what she really wanted to do if she wasn't in these streets like this. She said she wanted to go back to school, maybe be a teacher or some shit. So guess what, me and her had plans to go check out Buffalo State next week. See how we could make that happen. Monica was too smart to let this be her end game. I wouldn't let both of us end up like that. See, I said I would show her actions, not just words.

The party was boomin'. We were in full effect. Anika had all three ballrooms open. There were 3 different DJ's spinning the latest hits. They had everything from rap, to R&B and Reggae. Every nigga in there was family. It was drama free. Everyone paying homage to Anika and Que. Anika had announced at dinner that The Board of The FAM had approve her request to Co Rule the family operation with Que. So officially as of today, Que and Anika ruled as King and Queen. I respected that move. Anika didn't have to give up her title. Business was doing good and she had the support and respect from everyone. But that's that love shit. Anika didn't want to do this without Que. That's some real shit right there. Like I said before them two was the exception to the rule. They had a nigga, all of us, tryna find our Anika. Had us all thinking a nigga needed love in this game. When the truth was, we did. We all need an end game and for Que it was Anika and the boys.

The party was jammin. I was too cool for all that dancing shit, but I two stepped and allowed Monica to work me. Song after song we stayed on the floor or up in VIP dancing. I would do anything to see her smile. It was the least I could do. Most of the girls there couldn't hold a light to Monica. She looked like a new car on display at the dealer. You know the one you must save, steal and rob to get. Well I was on my way to having it. She was worth the wait. And every nigga in the spot knew it.

Que

Anika had out done herself. She had a nigga in his feelings. First the dinner and the news. I had no idea that she was going to do that. I would never ask her to give up her seat as the head of The FAM. She was doing such a great job, plus I had her back. I wouldn't allow her to fail. I guess that's why I loved her. She always did have a giving heart. I knew from that moment forward we were unstoppable. She was my Queen in every way. Lord knows I did not deserve her. She was the perfect distraction to the life we lead. And tonight, she had captured everyone's attention, mines included.

Anika and I danced in the VIP section. The bottles flowed. Everyone came over to say a few words to us. We were hood royalty. The King and Queen. It was one of the few times I let my guard down. Anika had a way of making me feel safe, which was funny, because that was my role for her. She provided the calm and collectedness with her presence. I adored the way Anika worked the crowd. Everyone respected her and there was not a female alive that didn't want to trade places with her. She was a vision. Anika looked amazing and as always, she was the center of attention.

Just when I thought the night could not get any better, Anika pulled me to the side. We were in a side room all alone. She handed me a small wrapped gift box. I felt cheated. I should have been giving her a gift for sticking by my side and being such an awesome mother to my sons in my absence. She just smiled and said, "Open it."

I stood there unraveling the bow and then taking off the wrapping paper. I could tell Anika was becoming impatient with me and my shenanigans. But, I took my time. If she could take the time to get me a gift, wrap it and present it to me, thnn I could take the time to appreciate the thought. I finally got to the white plain box. I looked up at Anika and whispered thank you as I opened it.

Inside was a silver spoon with a pink bow tied around the handle. It had an inscription engraved on it that read "Daddy's Little Girl". I paused and then looked at Anika. I paused again and looked at the spoon and then back at Anika.

"Oh Shit, Oh Shit!" I yelled out loud as I grabbed her and held her in my arms. "Oh shit" I yelled out again.

"Is this what I think it means?" I asked with excitement.

Anika shook her heads as if to say yes.

I swung her around in my arms and kissed her beautiful face. I stopped only to reach down and touch her belly. I kneeled in front of her and rested my head against her tummy.

"I'm twenty weeks today. It was so hard keeping this from you. With everything that we had going on and then Aaron... It just never seemed to be a good time. So I wanted to tell you tonight while we were celebrating. I wanted to give you a reason to keep smiling and look toward our future. I know you can't promise me anything, nor do I want you to. But know this, your legacy will continue and soon we will be adding a new member to the Thomas clan. I love you Quincey Lamont Thomas, I always have, and I always will."

She said as she rubbed my head while I rested on her listening to the sounds coming from her tummy.

"I know Anika, I know." I whispered, "And I love you more baby." I replied.

It was the new beginning I didn't know I needed. I had done a lot of shit in my time. Seen a lot of stuff I can't undo and made choices I'll have to live with. But there is one thing I was certain of... I had married the only person that could make me want to be a better man. I know I couldn't promise her certain things because of the lifestyle we live, but I promised myself, I would fight tooth and fuckin nail to get back to her and my family every night. I would protect them with my last breath.

After a few minutes alone we made our way back to the ballroom where all the action was. I walked with Anika up to the DJ booth and asked for a moment. All three ballrooms went silent. I thanked our family and friends for coming to party with us. I appreciated the warm welcome that everyone gave me for my homecoming. I thanked my two brothers in crime, Jay and Sleepy. I thanked my sisters in crime Monica and Yazz.

Lastly, but most importantly, I thanked my wife for her patience, love and loyalty.

"Anika, I could not be me without you" I said,

"You make a hood nigga wanna do somethin" I jokingly said making her blush.

And then I added, "And just a few minutes ago Anika shared with me that I was going to be a dad again. Our little princess will be here soon! I shouted"

The crowd went wide. The glasses clinked and there were roars of congratulation filled the air.

Once again Anika had made a nigga wanna be a man. She had filled me with so much hope that an exit game plan was a must. There was no way I wanted this for my family. I knew a lot of niggas that left the game usually by force. I had to make it so that I left the game on my terms. I needed to make sure I would be there for Anika, my boys and my unborn daughter. I had to be the man she.. they needed to be.

Jay

I watched Yazz and that dress all night. She was my equal in every way. She could be gentle and kind, but a bad ass all in one. That dress was killer, and it made me want to do things to her. The way she moved in that dress was sexy as hell. When we danced, she pressed her body up against mine. It was like the good ole days when she would freak me on the dance floor at some club. Except now, I had the grown and sexy version of my girl. And there was a lot of grown and sexy things I wanted to do to her.

I mingled through the crowd, but I spent most of my time in VIP overlooking the festivities. I tried to stay focused on Que and Anika. I needed to make sure they were good. And yes, I know it's not my job anymore, but they were my family and you always looked after family. This didn't stop me from surveying the crowd and being able to watch Yazz. I watched her dance, I watched her work the crowd and then I saw something that made me feel some kind of way.

I watched an encounter with Yazz and some dude that looked familiar. It was a small exchange, but it did not feel right to me. I couldn't hear what was said, I didn't notice what I would call flirtatious behavior on her part. I was all in the eyes. He gazed a few seconds too long and she refused to make eye contact. It looked just as weird as it felt. Yazz never backed down from anyone. Not looking someone in the eyes was not normal for her. I saw her cower. I saw her reject the opportunity to speak her strength with someone she could easily dominate. I was a quick glance and a brief encounter, but there was a story behind it. One I sure was going to ask about.

I excused myself from VIP. I saw the look Que gave me. I shook my head as if to say I'm good. He nodded. That was the beauty of our brotherhood; the nonverbal communication. I knew him and he knew me. We could read the clues and in between the lines and move accordingly. I knew he would be watching as I walked about. I knew that even when we weren't right next to each other he wasn't too far behind. He had my back and that was my man fifty grand. And even in a room full of family, there was still snakes in the muthafuckin grass. I think I spotted the snake and I was going to chop the head off.

Chapter Forty
"How You Gonna Act Like That "- Tyrese

Jay

All I knew was I swung off on the nigga. He tried it and I shut that shit down. Once I started swinging and he fell to the floor, there were family members around, who joined in. We stumped that nigga to his core. Even Que had made his way down to the dance floor and got a few jabs in. Security came and broke everything up. Once Reggie was on his feet, my reaction lead me to pull out my 9mm and put it in his face.

"Say something now Nigga" I warned. "Tell me to say hi to Yazz again" I commanded.

But he didn't say a word. He could barely stand on his own. His eyes were puffy and there was blood coming out of everywhere. I wanted to pull the trigger, but that nigga was a cop. He was on the take, but he was still a cop and as much as I wanted to blast that nigga's brains all over the back splash of the bar, Que, Yazz and my conscience would not allow me to. But my ego and pride had pulled the trigger.

I stormed out of the Club. I was heated and my thoughts had gone to a negative place. My emotions were being held captive on a rollercoaster. I paced back and forth trying to make sure that I had heard him correctly. I had rewound to the look on Yazz's face as I questioned her. I stood there watching her reaction and his reaction. I found myself wanting to kill them both. I felt the steam inside me raising and I just could not contain myself. I paced back and forth hot as hell. I asked the valet to bring me my car.

I needed to get the fuck out of there before I did something I would regret.

I sat there in the dark living room…alone. I was sippin' on some Christian Brothers. I heard Teddy Pendergrass and The Isley Brothers play softly in the background. I had no words and yet had so much to say. I just couldn't understand how and why. Maybe it was not meant for me to understand. Maybe I just needed to accept things for what they were. Maybe I've been playing the fool for way too long. Shid, maybe you can't make things the way they used to be. They say a good girl gone bad is a girl gone forever and that's just what I got. Maybe that was my punishment. Maybe that is what I get for taking something so precious and corrupting it. I know it was more the liquor controlling my thoughts than logic. It was the only way I knew how to mask the pain of what Yazz had done. It was the only way for me to feel better.

It was about two in the morning before she walked her nasty ass in the front door. I sat there watching her fumble her way inside. Somehow, she looked different. Like the rosy colored glasses I saw her through were gone. I had removed them, and I could see her clear as day. I don't know if it was the alcohol or if it was just me seeing her for what she had really become. I knew she was not the woman I had fallen in love with. Hell, she wasn't even the woman I had rescued from hell not so long ago. She was just a common bitch. You know the kinda bitch that lies and tries to cover shit up to suit their needs, the kind that says what she needs to say to get her way, suck a little dick and then have her hands out for payment of services. She was common and there was no way I could be in love with someone that was rooted in evil.

She wasn't even going to tell me about this shit. So here I am looking like a damn fool. In front of everyone. Had me thinking that WE could get things back to the way we were. Had a nigga thinking about puttin a ring on her finger and giving her my last name. This bitch had me, fooled me and played me for the joker. Bet she laughed at me every chance she got. I watched her taking off her shoes. YEAH, I bet I was the bunt of all her jokes. I thought lifting my glass to take another sip. The ice in the glass made a sound that echoed and notified Yazz that I was in the room with her. She made her way over to the light fixture by the side of the chair. She turned it on.

I sat there starring at her. There was nothing sexy about her anymore. I could not find one thing I wanted in her anymore. She was damaged goods. She stood there looking at me in silence.

"Jay we need to talk" Yazz spoke slyly.

"I don't have shit to say to you Yazz." I said as Teddy P's "The Whole Town's Laughing" played in the background.

"Jay, I'm so sorry. I did not mean for that to happen. I was afraid and scared that I had lost you to that other girl. I wasn't thinking at all. I don't know why I did it. It didn't mean anything baby" she said as she began to cry.

I watched with no emotion. Usually I would rush to her side and comfort her, but how do you comfort someone that doesn't have a heart.

There was a long pause where the only sounds where Stephanie Mills and Teddy's duet and Yazz's sobs.

"Jay, please say something. I love you baby" she cried.

"You love me, and you fuck him right?" I said taking a sip of my drink.

It wasn't like that "Yazz replied.

"Then how the fuck was it like Yazz. All those days with no visit from you. All those sleepless nights I worried about you. All those times during the past eighteen months when I was locked up and the only thing I wanted was you. All I wanted was for you to be ok. You was so worried about me fucking around on you and you out there fucking random niggas by accident. Is that what that was an accidental fuck? Tell me this, when you fucked him in the bathroom of that bar, were you thinking of me then too, because you sure as hell was on the visitor's list at the jail." I barked at her throwing my glass against the wall watching it shatter and its liquid content splash against it.

I had risen to my feet and was standing face to face with her. The tears flowed down her face like I had left the faucet on. There was a small part of me that felt bad for Yazz. I caught myself wanting to wipe her tears away. But I held back.

'I'm so sorry Jay, I'm so sorry," She whispered.

'How sorry are you Yazz?" I asked

"Baby I'll never do anything like that again. I never meant to hurt you, hurt us."

"How sorry are you Yazz?" I asked again.

"I'll do anything to make it up to you," She pleaded

Bingo, just what I wanted to hear.

"Take that dress off." I commanded. She obeyed.

I grabbed her into me. I unzipped my pants and pulled my half hard dick out, I slid her panties to the side and stuck my manhood int her.

I whispered "Fuck me like you did him,"

Yazz cried, but she fucked me.

With every tear she bounced that ass on my dick as I tried to strangle her with my grip on her neck. I slapped her ass as she grunted and moaned. I tried my damnest to break her, but she wouldn't cave. I could feel the tears dripping down her neck and onto my fingers. I yanked at her Hair as I ponded her pussy. I was desperately trying to reclaim something I no longer wanted. I fucked her and she fucked me back. Not once did I kiss her or say a word. I breathed my alcohol laced breath all over her body. Right before I came, I pushed her off me grabbed her hair turned her around on her knees and allowed her to drink the last serving of my cum. There was no way in hell I was going to release my seed into her. She was no longer worthy to be the mother of my children. I could not take that chance. She drank every drop as she cried even harder.

I just looked at her. No emotions. I just pitied her. She wasn't the queen of my heart any longer, just a street queen with no more aspirations than that. She was common and I saw her for what she was.

I pulled my pants up and watched her as she sat on the floor. I didn't say a word. The effects of the alcohol had worn off. My sober self was mad at my drunk self for what had transpired. But they both agreed on one ting, this house was not a home and we no longer wanted to be here. I grabbed my jacket and my keys. I took one final look at Yazz. It was an imagine I could not un-see. She looked weak, and damaged. Even though I played a part in her demise, she played an even greater role in the destruction of us. I would have helped her heal. But I can't fix my heart and hers. The damage was done and so was I and I walked out the door.

"Jay… Jay.. Jay please come back" She cried

I almost turned around.

"Please Jay.. "she begged

And all I could think was were was that love and need for me when I was locked up, better yet when you was fuckin ole' boy.

I picked up the pace, got in the car, put the keys in the ignition and drove away from the poison I had caused.

Chapter Forty-One
"Officially Missing You" –Tamia

Monica

It was days like this that brought a smile to my face. The streets were quiet for once. It didn't mean that something wasn't on the horizon, it just meant it was quiet. I had time to think. Time to relax and just let my guard down. Having Sleepy in my corner was a plus. He made everything ok. He brought the fun and excitement back into my life. I didn't think I would smile again. I also didn't think that I would find someone I could see myself with after Mario. I had all this before. Mario was my soulmate. He gave me the energy I needed. He was the first guy that truly knew me and accepted me for who I was, the good, bad and the ugly. He knew all that and he still loved me.

Mario and Sleepy were the same and yet so different. No, I'm not comparing, just simply stating facts. Mario was street for life. His biggest dream was being right where he was. He never saw himself doing or being anything other than a drug dealer. He knew he would live and die on these streets. In my heart I knew it too. But a piece of me wanted him to live for me, for us. But Mario loved me second to the streets and that was fine with me. At least I wasn't second to no bitch. With Sleepy on the other hand, I was first. He didn't say that I was, it was in the things he did. His actions screamed it. I loved that about him.

Mario and I were boyfriend and girlfriend. We walked around like an old school Bonnie and Clyde. I would cause the drama and he would scoop in and fuckin set the record straight. I loved it. I was just as crazy as him. It was the wild, wild west with us on the streets. Sleepy and I were different. We didn't have labels, at least not yet. But he treated me like I was his. We agreed to take thing slow. Sleepy said he wouldn't share me with any other nigga, we had to be in a monogamist relationship. Shid, the way he dicked me down, I didn't crave anyone else. But I did miss the threesomes with Mario and the way we would smoke the blunt and talk about sports and shit. With Sleepy we cuddled after sex and he asked me questions about life and what I wanted. My dreams and my future. It made me think about my goals before all this started. Before my heart was ever broken, when I had hope and hadn't seen the things I did or done the shit I've done.

Sleepy wasn't the thug nigga everyone thought he was. Yeah, he was street and he was rough around the edges, but there was gentler side of him. The side he only shared with me. Like he could cook. I mean really cooked. He could sing, and deep down I think he believed in love, just not that romantic shit you see in white folks movies, but that hood love. He was a complete gentleman when dealing with me. It gave me hope, he gave me hope. I liked the person I was becoming with him. It was like he had tamed me, and I was no longer the wild child that roamed the streets. He had taught me the game and allowed me to be a partner. He trusted me and I knew I was safe with him. There was something happening between us and I knew it was bigger than what we both thought.

Everyone wanted to know what was happening between us. Sleepy and I said this thing we got goin on was between me and him. Letting the world in is what messes things up. He said no one should have to ask, they should be able to see that he was mines and I was his. That there was some deep shit. He promised me no girl would ever bring some shit about him to me. He said he had respected me that much. Besides, even if they did I would shut that shit down. I guess everyone was noticing everything that I've grown to know. Sleepy's actions showed his true intentions and needless to say I was at the top of the list of his priorities. But It didn't mean that I didn't miss Mario and the fun we had. Sometimes I just wanted to be Bonnie, but my Clyde was gone.

Chapter Forty-Two
"Complicated" - Robin Thicke

Yazz

It had been two months since I last saw Jay. One day, I left out to handle some business and when I returned later that night all of Jay's things were gone. He left his keys and a small jewelry box that had a diamond engagement ring in it. I should have cried, but I was all cried out. I knew I had hurt him. I wasn't sure it was on purpose or if subconsciously I did what I did as an act of revenge. Me fuckin' Reggie didn't mean shit. I wanted to and I let him. It was that simple. Did I wish he was Jay, no. I think a piece of me wanted to hold on to the thought of us. We had been together for so long it just seemed like it had to be us.

But what I learned in therapy was sometimes the love of two people is only supposed to last for a season. Jay and my time had outlived its season. We are poison for each other, a beautiful fire of destruction, setting everything in our path a blaze and then wishing the cup of water we each had could put out the flames. I didn't blame him or leaving, I just wish we had ended things on a better note. There was no reason for me to pass on my baggage to him. It was mines and mines alone to carry. I know that now. But my fear is that I handed him my broken heart tote and he had it on his back now. Did I miss Jay. Everyday. And everyday things got a little easier. And I hurt a little less.

I remember what Que said when we all met that day at the prison. He told us to either fix it or let it go. I didn't hear hm then or understand his words, but Jay and I were bad for business. We were messing up. And someone was going to get hurt if we kept going at that speed. I certainly did not want that on my conscious and I know he didn't either. It was for the best, at least that was what I wanted to believe. Besides, Jay moved to North Carolina. Que told me he was down there taking care of business for him for a while. It didn't mean he wouldn't return. Que said Jay needed some space. I thought I would see him in passing, but he cut me off cold turkey. And the withdraws killed me for a while. My rehab said one day at a time. So, the memories of him will have to do.

I was keeping busy. The streets never sleep and with my restless nights I needed so stay focused. I rode solo. I was still Anika's right hand and I was slowly earning Que's favor again. Every once in a while Jay would call while I was over there. We never spoke, but I could hear small traces of his voice echo through the phone. He sounded good. It would make me smile on the inside. All I ever wanted was the best for him and I hoped he knew that.

I kept to myself. I handled business and worked on me. That was the best I could do for now. I would hope and pray that one day I wouldn't be so complicated. Wait what the hell. I'd always be complicated I just needed a nigga that would be ok with my complicities, that he would look at me like a great work of art and admire my intricate designs and brush strokes and love me for who I was and not for what or who he wanted me to be. Yeah, I was one complicated bitch and I was learning to love her. I was figuring it out and all the pieces to my puzzle fit perfectly perfect.

Chapter Forty-Three

"No Idea's Original" – Nas

Que

It had been almost five months since my release. Everything was back to normal. I had my family and that was all that mattered. Anika's belly was growing daily. She was almost ready to deliver. The excitement was growing in the house. The twins kept asking when the baby was coming, and Anika had done enough shopping that this little girl shouldn't need anything until she was twenty. I was just happy we could do it right this time. No drama, no stress, and no lies. This is what I would have pictured if I had allowed myself to have a future like the one I've created. This life I lead, this false sense of security that I've created for myself had me living in a world most drug dealers never get or see or imagine.

Business was good. The hustle never stops. There was always a corner to protect, money to make and someone who thinks they can come up on your block. The streets were changing and so was the way we did business. Anika was way ahead of her time with what she did to try to legitimize the organization. We were looking like a real company. We had moved a lot of the operation off the streets. With a new mayor who promised to clean up the streets and stop the corruption in the police force, we needed to stay ahead of his moves. Yeah we still had people on the take, but this new nigga was different. It was going to take a minute before I could figure him out. Either way, we needed to stay off the radar. And just because the streets were changing, didn't mean that me and Anika ruled with a soft hand. She might be pregnant, but she was still a force. And me, I was always going to be that nigga.

Expansion was going well. With Jay out in the territory tightening up shit and making our presence felt, it was business as usual. I missed my brother. Not having him here by my side is different. The twins missed Uncle Jay. But he called weekly and spoke to them. I would ask him about him and Yazz and he would change the subject. I reminded him that running from shit never solved anything. He would then say something slick and get me going. But I get it, you need peace of mind and calmness. This life we lead if Jay needed to leave to get that clarity, then I'mma support that nigga. After all I was my brother's keeper, whether he was right here by my side or five states away; distance was just a number, but that bond was solid and could and would conquer time and distance.

I was still working on that exist plan. I had too. When the time was right I would let Anika know we needed to step down. Hopefully that would be before we had to explain to the boys the life we live. There was no way I wanted this for the twins or my daughter. Like I said before the streets were changing. The last thing I needed was for them to get caught up in some fuck shit and everything I worked for, everything I worked so hard to protect would bring the streets right back into our home. We did our best to keep that outside of these walls. Inside of these walls on this street, we were just the Thomas's nothing more nothing less. But the minute we stepped out of that door we could be whatever the fuck we needed to be to protect this. I planned to keep it that way, and if I had my way, we would just be the Thomas's all the time. Until then I'd work on that plan and try to wipe my feet at the door so the streets don't sneak into the house by accident.

Chapter Forty-Four
"Stay Down"- Mary J Blige

Anika

I loved Sunday dinners. It was the one time I knew I would see the people that I loved. Every Sunday no exceptions. Everyone better have their asses at the dining room table. Sleepy, Monica, and Yazz. Jay would call and it felt like we were all together. The boys were three and growing up so fast and Asia was a handful. She was almost one. Que had spoiled that girl. She was truly a daddy's girl. All of us at the table. Catching up on shit. We never talked business. That time was reserved for just us. What was going on in our lives, sports, jokes and shit talk. This was my family. It was the one I built. We had each been through enough and through it all, we had each other's backs fronts and sides. I loved each and every one of them.

I was so proud of Monica for going back to school. Who would have thought she'd be a teacher. Lord help them kids. Her ass wouldn't hesitate to yoke a kid up, I thought to myself laughing out loud. Her and Sleepy were still doing them. I wasn't sure what to call them, and the more I thought about them the less I cared. They loved each other and they were positive influences on each other. Don't get me wrong, they both were still thugs at heart, but considering the world we navigate through, finding someone who understands the struggle, the danger and the chaos was limited. Yet they had each other. I was happy for them and when we were together I could feel Mario's spirit smiling down on them and us.

I still worried about Yazz. I always thought she and Jay would find a way to work it out. But last year we received an invitation from Jay to attend his wedding. Que was the best man. It was a beautiful wedding and Shawntrice is a really nice girl. I thought when I told Yazz that she would have lost it. She told me that Jay had called her and told her himself. When I asked her how she felt about it, she shrugged her shoulders and walked away. Her eyes said it all though. I asked her if she wanted to ride down there and handle that shit and get her man back and she just said she was happy for him. I think deep down she meant it. I just wanted Yazz to find someone who would love her and help her love herself. I know this life can do things to you. I prayed she'd find her happy ever after or at least just be happy.

The only person missing was Ayanna. Oh, how I missed my sister. I know she's smiling down on us. I find myself talking to her all the time. I show the boys her and Mario's pictures often. I want them to know who their Auntie and Uncle are and how special they were to me and Que. I wish I could hear your voice one more time. Or see your smile or even clown with you again. We all could use your motherly love right about now. I pray none of us see you soon, but if one of us had to, I know you and Mario would take good care of them. I miss you sis, and yes, I'll love everyone for you. I get that mothering shit from you.

Where do I even begin. My life isn't perfect by any means, buy it's all mine. I have a husband I love with my whole being. He's been my headache, my hero, my friend, my lover, my boss, the father of my children and my god. Sometimes I find myself looking at him like I did when I was a kid. You know that starry eyed schoolgirl crush look. I watch him walk into a room and I still get goose bumps. He has given me everything and then some. I pray for his return home every night and day. I pray that he finds peace in this crazy world we live. It's almost like we live a lie. I know at any time it can all end, but it was worth the gamble. It was worth the sacrifice just to get to this point.

The streets are the streets. They claim more lives than they should. Everyday some youngin' makes the choice to enter into this world. And every day a mother loses her dream. I made the same choice. Walked those same steps and now that I'm a mother I wouldn't wish this on anyone. Yes, I live it, I've seen too much and done things I have to live with, but if I can change the narrative for my sons, God, give me the strength and power to do so. I pray we never have to explain any of this to them. I pray they never see Que and I on visitation day locked behind bars and concrete. I pray they never have the blood on their perfect hands the way we do. I pray and hope my pleas don't fall on God's deaf ears. I made choices so that they don't have to. I know very few leave this world on their own accord, I pray we all are among the few. I pray for Mario and Ayanna to guard over my family and do their part to keep us safe.

I chose both, the streets and love. Que chose both. Yazz chose the streets, but she wanted both. Monica didn't really chose one or the other and Jay wanted love but the streets chose him. It's a tricky game we played. Each choice had consequences. Consequences we all have to live with. I just pray the choices get easier and the actions reap rewards instead of punishments. The streets of Buffalo NY ain't no joke. The hood will eat you up and spit you out. But with friends like my girls and the guys we have in our corners, the bruises weren't so bad. We had fun, but we also had our share of drama. Lord I hope the boys make better choices. I hope Asia finds love anywhere but where her mother did. Lord help us if the cycle continues.

THE 716
The Next Generation

"Meet Me At the London"- Young Thug (ft J.Cole, Travis Scott)

Rockmond

"The bitches up in here looking like they IG ready," I said to Dray and my boy Money. We drove into the city. It was Friday night and hell, it was graduation night. We couldn't be any more lit than we were. We just finished high school and all three of us were getting ready to head off to college. I was going to Buffalo State University to play Basketball. Yup ya boy was part of a highly recruited class. Buff State had been doing their thing the past few years. They wasn't even on my radar, but when they made it to the tournament, I gave them a look. Then when the coach came to the house, moms was all excited. They talked a good game. So why not. Plus, it got me in the city. I hate living out in the boonies. I wanted to be around niggas that looked like me. Smoked weed like me and partied like me. So tonight, I was cuttin' the fuck up.

"Ballin"-Mustard (ft Roddy Ricch)

Draymond

"Shit baby suck that dick slow, yeah like that. Work that shit baby. Work those angles for the camera." I said as I watched Shay and Michelle fight over who was going suck my dick better. I was capturing every lick split and twerk on my iPhone.

There was a knock at my dorm room door. Niggas always hating. I know they saw the sign on the door. I tried ignoring whoever it was, but they kept banging on the door.

"Who the fuck is it," I screamed as I opened the door with my towel around my waist.

Only thing I saw was the end of a gun barrel……….

"Omen" – The Lox

Que

I got the call form one of the soldiers in the city. I was driving like a bat out of hell. "Fuck! Ray and Dray," I screamed out as I hit the steering wheel. "What the fuck were yall up too?" I said out loud.

The screen on the dashboard read Jay. I answered the call.

"Jay, I need you brother." I commanded.

"What's going on?" Jay asked.

"It's the twins.." I responded.

"Say no more, I'm on the next flight out." Jay confirmed.

The phone went dead. "Goddamnit! These little niggas are about to learn a lesson the hard way. I better get to them before Anika finds out or we all gonna have hell to pay."